T0149452

# TOWARDS
# A
# VIABLE
# MONETARY
# SYSTEM

# TOWARDS A VIABLE MONETARY SYSTEM

The Need for a National Complementary
Currency for the United States

## HUSSAIN ZAHID IMAM

# TOWARDS A VIABLE MONETARY SYSTEM
# THE NEED FOR A NATIONAL COMPLEMENTARY
# CURRENCY FOR THE UNITED STATES

iUniverse books may be ordered through booksellers or by contacting:

iUniverse
1663 Liberty Drive
Bloomington, IN 47403
www.iuniverse.com
1-800-Authors (1-800-288-4677)

Library of Congress Control Number: 2017913331

ISBN: 978-1-5320-3220-2 (sc)
ISBN: 978-1-5320-3219-6 (e)

Print information available on the last page.

iUniverse rev. date: 08/29/2017

# CONTENTS

# PART III

# PREFACE

For almost ten years, ever since the financial crisis of 2007-2008, I have been thinking, reading, researching, and wondering about our monetary system. The reasons for the financial crises that have occurred have been researched and analyzed by many scholars, and many ideas about how to reform the current monetary system have been proposed, but all of these monetary reform proposals involve the wholesale replacement of the current monetary system of the United States.

The replacement of the private, fractional reserve banking system with a nationalized, 100% reserve banking system is neither politically possible, nor is it really necessary to completely replace it. In fact, for reasons that are explained in this book, it would be unwise to replace a private single currency system with another nationalized single currency system.

In 1933, the Chicago Plan called for abolishing fractional reserve banking, but we do not need to abolish fractional reserve banking at the present time, for the purpose of preventing the next financial or economic crisis. As I have explained in detail in this book, we can keep private fractional banking and the Federal Reserve System exactly like it is, and still be able to ward off the threat of the next financial crisis.

After ten years of thinking and researching, I am now convinced that I have found the solution to the threat posed by the unsustainable burden of interest on our national debt, which will most likely be the cause of the next financial or economic crisis.

It has taken me six months to write this book, and I am so glad to have finally finished writing it. I realize that time is of the essence, because if we are not able to pay the interest due on the federal debt, we will be in default on the national debt. According to the Congressional Budget Office, the interest payment on the national debt will be $714 billion in the year 2026.

There is absolutely no way that the single currency monetary system currently in place in the U.S. monetary system can deal with the impending disaster of a debt default all by itself. However, if another demurrage charged electronic currency is established through monetary reform, and allowed to coexist in parallel with the conventional U.S. dollar, then we will be able to solve the problem of unsustainable interest payments, and a debt default can be averted.

My motivation in writing this book is to explain to the people of the United States how it is possible to avert the possibility of a default on the national debt through the introduction of a second currency which will serve as a backup if the first currency fails. A currency that exists independently as a parallel currency is called a complementary currency.

After earning a B.Sc.Honors Degree in First Class from the University of Dhaka in Bangladesh, I came to the United States as a student and earned an MBA degree in 1978. I started my own business after finishing my education, and currently my wife Fatima and myself own and operate a gasoline station in Athens, Georgia. Without my wife Fatima's help, support, and encouragement, this book would not have been possible.

While at work at this gasoline station, I have been thinking, reading, researching, and wondering, for the last ten years, about a viable monetary system for the United States. I wrote this book while working at my place of business. I tried my best to write this book in plain and simple language, without the use of technical jargon, so that people without a background in economics or banking may find it easy to understand the contents of this book.

I became a naturalized U.S. citizen on June 5, 1991. As a United States citizen, I hope that the dual currency monetary reform proposed in this book will help the people of the United States in avoiding another financial, monetary, or economic crisis. If it does, then all the hard work that has gone into researching and finally writing this book, will not have been in vain.

# INTRODUCTION

The cause of the 2007- 2008 financial crisis which threatened to bring down the entire financial system can be debated endlessly, but it is more important now to focus on the possible causes of the next financial crisis. What can cause the next financial crisis? It appears that the possibility of a default on the national debt by the U.S. government poses the most serious threat of triggering a financial crisis.

Unless something is done to reduce the unsustainable burden of interest on the national debt, there is a real possibility of a default on Treasury debt by the U.S. government. It seems that the next financial crisis will be precipitated by a default on the federal debt, and this default cannot be prevented with the single conventional currency currently in place in the existing monetary system of the United States.

Monetary reformers want to eliminate privately issued bank money and replace it with publicly issued money, but nationalizing the banking industry will not eliminate the problem of growing interest payments which is fast becoming unsustainable. Monetary reformers want to abolish fractional reserve banking and replace it with 100% reserve money. Even if it were politically possible to abolish fractional reserve banking, abolishing fractional reserve banking would not, by itself, remove the unsustainable burden of interest on the national debt.

Fractional reserve banking may have its flaws, but it has at least one undeniable advantage in that a bank can create money that has a higher velocity than the velocity of the rest of the money stock. Proof of this lies in the fact that in the second quarter of 2017, the velocity of M1 money

1

stock was 5.528, whereas the velocity of M2 money stock was 1.425. If fractional reserve banking is abolished, there would not be enough money with sufficient velocity in it to produce the exchange of goods and services in the economy.

Because of the nature of the conventional dollar which plays the dual role of a medium of exchange and the role of a store of value, interest paid by banks to depositors does not necessarily cause depositors to spend their interest income. In stark contrast, interest paid by borrowers to banks is only possible if borrowers are able to earn the money to pay interest through economic activity. Thus, interest paid by banks to depositors basically results in money that becomes a store of value as the interest income is added to the savings accounts of those depositors. Diametrically opposed to this function as a store of value, money received as interest income by banks from borrowers is money that has been playing the role of a medium of exchange, because borrowers had to earn this money to pay interest by toiling hard to exchange their goods and services.

Savers accumulate interest income from their savings accounts, their certificates of deposit, their negotiable orders of withdrawal, and their money market accounts, to add to the preexisting hoards of their savings. Banks do not accumulate interest income from borrowers to serve as a store of value. Their job is to lend money to earn more interest. Money that comes to a bank as interest is more likely to be lent again and then spent, as opposed to money that a saver receives as interest income, which is less likely to be spent, and more likely to be saved.

Interest income that flows to savers from financial institutions may be good in so far as the individual savers are concerned, but is not necessarily good for the economy as a whole, because such a flow of interest income removes money that is circulating as a medium of exchange in the economy, and adds to the stockpile of money that is primarily serving as a store of value.

When someone borrows money from a bank, the purpose is to make money with the borrowed money. No one borrows money at a higher rate of interest from a bank to put this money in a savings account at a lower rate of interest. Money that is loaned into existence is money that is guaranteed to circulate, because the borrower has no choice but to put this money to work, if the intention is to repay the loan with interest.

This cannot be said of money that is spent into the economy, which stops circulating once it passes into the hands of those who can afford to save it, rather than spend it.

As of July 17, 2017, there were $1.3838 trillion in demand deposits and $11.505 trillion in savings deposits, certificates of deposits, NOW accounts, and other money market accounts. The demand deposits of $1.3838 trillion constituted only 10 percent of the total money supply of M2 which was $13.6083 trillion. The amount of M1, that is, coin + cash + demand deposits + travelers checks, was $3.4867 trillion on July 17, 2017. Thus, the money supply represented by M1 was only about 25% of the money supply represented by M2 on July 17, 2017.

According to the website of the Board of Governors of the Federal Reserve System, there were $1.3838 trillion dollars in demand deposits as of July 17, 2017. There seems to be a belief that if all bank debt money is repaid, the entire money supply will vanish. This belief is a misconception because if all demand deposits of $1.3838 trillion were repaid on July 17, 2017, there would still have been $13.6083 - $1.3838 = $12.445 trillion of money left in the economy on July 17, 2017. It is true that the velocity of M1 money stock is far greater than the velocity of M2 money stock, but the undeniable fact is that the entire money supply of the economy will not become zero if all bank debt money is paid back.

If a multimillionaire who has millions of dollars of his own money, lends a million dollars to a business, no money is lent into existence, because it is only a transfer of preexisting money from the multimillionaire to the business as a loan. No money will be destroyed when the business repays the one million dollar loan to the multimillionaire. The entire money stock represented by M2, is almost ten times the total amount of demand deposits in the economy, hence it is impossible for the entire money supply to be wiped out by repayment of all the loans that have been loaned into existence by banks through fractional reserve banking.

During the fiscal year 2015, the federal government spent a total of $3.9 trillion on health and human services, social security, defense, veteran affairs, and interest payments on Treasury securities. Dollars that are spent into the economy in the form of government spending do not circulate as much as dollars that are lent into the economy. As soon as dollars that are spent into the economy eventually circulate into the hands of those who prefer to save this money, the circulation of this money slows down considerably. For this reason, the ability of government spending to stimulate economic activity is limited in the current monetary system.

The velocity of M2 money stock was 1.776 in the first quarter of 1959, and after reaching a high of 2.210 in the third quarter of 1997, it has been steadily declining since then. At the end of the second quarter of 2017, the velocity of M2 money stock was 1.425. This reflects a decline of 35.6% in the velocity of M2 money stock in the two decades between 1997 and 2017.

The velocity of M1 money stock was 3.668 in the first quarter of 1959, and after climbing to a high of 10.688 in the fourth quarter of 2007, it has collapsed dramatically since then. At the end of the second quarter of 2017, the velocity of M1 money stock was 5.528. The velocity of M1 money stock fell by half in the decade from 2007 to 2017.

According to the website of the Federal Reserve Bank of St. Louis, in the second quarter of 2017, the velocity of M1 money stock was 5.528, whereas the velocity of M2 money stock was 1.425. This big difference in the velocities of M1 and M2 money stock means that M1, which is equal to coins + cash + demand deposits + travelers checks, is playing the predominant role as a medium of exchange in the economy, while the rest of the money stock represented by (M2 -M1) is mainly playing the role of a store of value. In the current monetary system, the exchange of goods and services depends on checking account money far more than it does on that part of the money supply that is represented by (M2 - M1). Repayment of all bank debt money will not erase the money supply, but it will certainly reduce the exchange of goods and services because the stock of higher velocity money will be removed from the money supply.

Because bank debt money is performing a vital service in the current monetary system by providing a high velocity money stock, does this mean that we must remain permanently dependent on money that has been borrowed into existence as debt? As long as bank debt money is the only source of high velocity money stock, we have no choice but to continue to borrow money into existence because that is the only way we can have money stock with sufficiently high velocity in it, to cause the exchange of goods and services. Not only that, a growing economy needs a growing supply of high velocity money, not money with insufficient velocity. The alarming implication is that, in order to grow our economy within the parameters of the current monetary system, we must take on more debt, so that more bank debt money with sufficient velocity can be loaned into the economy.

To change this status quo, we need a dual currency monetary system with two currencies existing side by side, one of which is fundamentally different in nature to the conventional dollar. We need a complementary currency with a built in capability to speed up transactions. In other words, we need a demurrage charged currency that will supply the economy with money stock that has sufficient velocity in it, to produce the exchange of goods and services. This will reduce our dependence on money that has been borrowed into existence for the exchange of our goods and services, because private banks will not be allowed to lend Smart dollars into existence; only the Federal Reserve will create Smart dollars that can be spent or lent into the economy.

In the current single currency monetary system, the fraction of lower velocity money stock is much higher than that of higher velocity money stock in the total money supply of the economy. There is no monetary tool available to alter the proportion of higher velocity money stock in the money supply. The only possible way to boost the proportion of higher velocity money stock in the total money supply of the economy is through the introduction of a second currency which is fundamentally different in nature to the first currency.

U.S. dollars can be dropped from helicopters and collected by people as they fall on the ground, but there is no certainty that people who come into possession of this money will be spending it any time soon. They might prefer to save this money that fell into their hands from the sky. Unless this drop of money from the sky is spent, there will be no change in income, and consequently no increase in the nation's output of goods and services. Electronic demurrage money cannot be dropped from the sky by means of helicopters, but it can surely be credited electronically to an individual's demurrage checking account. An individual receiving this kind of money will be much more inclined to spend it on goods and services, before demurrage kicks in, and the money balance starts declining in the holder's demurrage checking account.

The velocity of circulation of money is the result of dividing the GDP by the money supply in the economy, that is, the GDP is the result of multiplying a given money stock by its velocity of circulation. If the money stock M2 remains unchanged, a declining velocity of M2 will produce a smaller GDP, whereas an increasing velocity of M2 will result in a higher GDP. Since the velocity of both M2 money stock and M1 money stock have declined by 35.6%, and 50% respectively over the last two decades, a higher GDP has only been possible over the last two decades by an increase in M2 money stock, with a concomitant rise in price inflation.

The decline in velocity of the traditional dollar in the current single currency monetary system is cause for serious concern, because the only way that the GDP of the U.S. economy can increase in future years in the face of declining velocity of its money stock, is through increases in its M2 money stock, which is inherently inflationary. The detrimental effect of declining velocity in a conventional single currency monetary system can be offset by the introduction of a demurrage charged complementary currency. As explained in detail in this book, a demurrage charged complementary currency will have a very high velocity of circulation, and if allowed to coexist in parallel with our traditional U.S. dollar, this demurrage currency will alleviate the harmful effects of declining velocity of conventional M1 and M2 money stock.

When bank debt money is loaned into existence by private commercial banks, only the principal amount of the loan is created as bank debt. Interest accumulates over a period of time, and so the accumulated interest at the time a loan is made is zero. It is impossible for a private bank to create the money needed for repayment of interest at the time of making the loan. Where does the money required to pay the interest on a bank loan come from?

Does the money to pay the interest necessarily have to come from the issuance of more loans as bank debt? The fact that the amount of demand deposits is not increasing as fast as M2 minus demand deposits, strongly suggests that interest payments on existing bank debt do not come from the issuance of additional bank debt money in the form of demand deposits. If banks had to loan money so that a new borrower's principal could fund an older borrower's interest, then the amount of demand deposits in the economy would have increased at a much faster rate than (M2 - demand deposits). Eventually, the total amount of demand deposits would equal

(M2 - demand deposits), and after that the amount of demand deposits would overtake the amount of (M2 - demand deposits). However, the fact of the matter is that the total amount of demand deposits was $1.3838 trillion on July 17, 2017, whereas the entire money stock represented by M2 was $13.6083 trillion on the same date, according to figures published on the website of the Federal Reserve System. Therefore, M2 minus demand deposits, was equal to $13.6083 - $1.3838 = $12.2245 trillion on July 17, 2017. This is irrefutable proof that the money to pay interest on bank debt does not come from the creation of more money as bank debt.

The interest needed to service bank loans comes from that part of the money supply that no longer needs to be repaid as debt. After being borrowed into existence, some bank debt money eventually circulates into the hands of people who do not need this money to repay debt, because these people are not debtors - their assets are greater than their liabilities. People with positive net worth own debt free assets and possess cash balances in savings accounts. When people with positive net worth spend money, they inject money into the economy which can be used to pay the interest on outstanding bank loans. The problem is that it is hard for people who need to pay interest to banks, to earn the money available in the hands of people with positive net worth, because in the single non demurrage currency in the monetary system of today, there is no incentive for people to spend. If a demurrage based complementary currency is allowed to coexist with the traditional U.S. dollar, it would be much easier for people with debt to earn the money to repay their debt.

If savers do not save money and make it available to banks, then where will banks get the money to lend to borrowers? Banks do not need the savings of depositors to lend to borrowers, nor does a bank wait for depositors to deposit their savings in bank accounts in order to make loans. If a credit worthy customer walks into a bank for a loan, and the bank wants to make the loan, it will create the money out of nothing to make the loan, and then arrange for adequate reserves at the Central bank. Whether you like it or not, this is the beauty of fractional reserve banking invented by Venetian bankers and goldsmiths several centuries ago, and now practiced by our modern private banking industry.

The beauty of fractional reserve banking to conjure money out of nothing is the underlying cause of its fragility and instability. It is fragile because a bank can only expand its lending at the same rate as other banks. There is no limit to the amount of money that a bank can loan into existence if it moves in step with other banks. A bank is weakened when it moves one step ahead of other banks in its rate of expansion of lending, but is strengthened when other banks move one step ahead of it in their rate of expansion of lending. If all banks expand their lending at the same rate, all banks are safe. The problem arises when a bank over expands its lending, leading to a net outflow of its central bank reserves at the central bank. When this happens, a private commercial bank will fail because although it can create demand deposits, it cannot create central bank reserves.

It costs nothing for a private commercial bank to create money, and this is the reason why some private banks are prone to making risky loans in search of higher profits. Since the banking system consists of banks that affect each other, the failure of one big bank or financial institution can threaten the stability of the entire financial system. This is exactly what happened in the financial crisis of 2007-2008.

The only way to avoid this vulnerability regarding the fragility and instability inherent in the one currency monetary system is to have a dual currency monetary system. A systemic failure in one part of a dual currency monetary system cannot bring down the whole edifice of a dual currency system. If fractional reserve banking fails, its failure cannot effect the operation of the complementary currency, because both currency systems will function independently of each other. In essence, a second currency will serve as a backup if the first currency fails.

There are three kinds of money in the current monetary system. The first is coin and currency, the second is central bank reserves that exist in electronic form only, and the third is money that is loaned into existence by private banks, known as demand deposits or checking account money. Coins, currency, and central bank reserves constitute the base money of the country, and can only be minted, printed, and created, respectively, by the Federal Reserve. It might seem that base money is privately issued money because Federal Reserve banks are private corporations, but the truth of the matter is that base money is, indeed, publicly issued money. Why is this so?

Although Federal Reserve banks are privately owned, base money is, in reality, publicly issued money because the Federal Reserve System is an arm of the United States government. The nominally private ownership of the twelve Federal Reserve banks, is a smokescreen that hides the fact that the Federal Reserve is a de facto branch of the U.S. government. The twelve Federal Reserve banks are federally chartered corporations, each with stockholders, directors, and a president, but the seven members of the Board of Governors of the Federal Reserve System are all appointed by the President with the aid and advice of the Senate.

The member banks of each of the twelve Federal Reserve banks are the stockholders of each Federal Reserve district bank, and each private commercial bank that is a member of the Federal Reserve bank must purchase an amount of stock that is equivalent to 3% of its capital and surplus. Dividend payments on this stock are limited to 6%. After deducting its costs from its income, and after paying the 6% dividends, a Federal Reserve bank must hand over all remaining profits to the U.S. Treasury. In January of 2016, the Federal Reserve said that it had sent $97.7 billion in profits to the U.S. Treasury for the year 2015. Does a private corporation that is truly private turn over most of its profits to the government?

The stockholders of each Federal Reserve bank select six of its nine directors, while the other three directors are appointed by the Board of Governors. The managing officials of the Federal Reserve bank in each district is appointed by the Board of Directors of each district bank, but the Board of Governors of the Federal Reserve System has a veto power over the selection of the managing officials. More often than not, the Federal Reserve Board has been instrumental in appointing the presidents of the twelve district banks.

Apart from the Board of Governors of the Federal Reserve System, the Open Market Committee is the other important policy body in the system. The members of the Open Market Committee are the seven governors of the Federal Reserve System, and the twelve district bank presidents. Only five of the district bank presidents can vote at any one time, which means that ultimate control lies in the hands of the Board of Seven Governors of the Federal Reserve System. Control of the Federal Reserve System is guaranteed to be in the hands of the United States government.

Despite the nominal private ownership of Federal Reserve banks, there should be no doubt that, for all practical purposes, the Federal

Reserve System is a branch of the U.S. government. Therefore, base money consisting of coins, currency, and electronic central bank reserves are publicly issued money. Only money that is lent into existence by private commercial banks, referred to as demand deposits, or checking account money, is privately issued money.

Abolishing fractional reserve banking and replacing it with 100% publicly issued money will not cause the problem of deficits to go away, nor will it eliminate the possibility of a default on the national debt if the U.S. Treasury is not able to pay the interest on the national debt which is growing by the hour, and is estimated by the Congressional Budget Office to reach $714 billion in the year 2026.

According to the Congressional Budget Office, at the close of the fiscal year of 2016 on September 30, 2016, the debt held by the public was $14.17 trillion, and intra governmental holdings amounted to $5.40 trillion. This total national debt of $19.57 trillion at the end of fiscal year 2016 did not include the so called "agency debt", which refers to the debt of federal agencies such as FHLB and GNMA, and of government sponsored enterprises, such as Fannie Mae and Freddie Mac.

In addition to the national debt of $19.57 trillion on September 30, 2016, the federal government had: 1) $8.54 trillion in liabilities such as federal employee retirement benefits, accounts payable, and environmental/ disposal expenses. 2) $29.04 trillion in obligations for current social security participants above and beyond projected revenues from payroll taxes and assets of the social security trust fund. 3) $32.90 trillion in obligations for current medicare participants above and beyond projected revenues from payroll taxes, benefit taxes, premium payments, and assets of the medicare trust fund. These unfunded obligations amounted to $70.48 trillion. If these unfunded obligations are added to the national debt of $19.57 trillion, the federal government had debts, liabilities, and unfunded obligations in the amount of $90.05 trillion on September 30, 2016.

What about the assets that the federal government currently owns? According to the report, Federal Assets Above and Below Ground, from the Institute for Energy Research, dated January 17, 2003, the U.S. government: 1) Owns more than 900,000 assets of real property with a combined area of 3 billion square feet. 2) Owns more than 600 million acres of onshore land, some with minerals underground. 3) Owns or manages approximately 755 million acres of onshore subsurface mineral estate. 4) Owns 1.76 billion acres of offshore mineral estate extending 200 nautical miles from the U.S. coast.

Obviously, the federal government owns a large mineral estate with huge reserves of crude oil, natural gas, and coal. This enormous mineral estate has an estimated value of over $150 trillion. If these resources are leased, the Congressional Budget Office conservatively estimates that the federal government could earn $150 billion over the next ten years in rents and royalties. $15 billion per year in rents and royalties from our enormous mineral estate is only a drop in the bucket when compared with the projected interest expense of $714 billion in the year 2026.

The federal government also owns $948 billion in outstanding federal student loans, and also possesses the largest hoard of gold in the world of about 261,498,926.230 troy ounces. At the market rate of $1,226.60 per troy ounce, this sizable stash of gold owned by the U.S. government was worth about $321 billion on August 6, 2017.

Tax revenue has fluctuated between 23% and 28% of GDP during the last fifteen years. Studies have consistently shown that an increase in tax rates do not lead to increases in tax revenue. Future interest payments on the national debt cannot be funded by generating more income taxes, nor can it be funded by rents and royalties received by leasing the entire mineral estate of the country. Even if the U.S. sells its entire stock of gold, the interest payment on the national debt cannot be paid.

An alternate source of income is required to fund future interest payments so that a default on the national debt can be avoided. Incredible as it may seem, such a new source of income is available to the U.S. government, if the U.S. government legislates into existence a demurrage charged national complementary currency, which we will affectionately call our 'Smart' dollar. Abolishing fractional reserve banking is not necessary, nor is nationalization of the current monetary system required, in order to establish a national complementary currency.

The services of the Federal Reserve System is crucial for a national complementary currency to operate in parallel with the traditional U.S. dollar. Just as the Federal Reserve creates central bank reserves of conventional U.S. dollars out of nothing by tapping numbers into a computer, it will similarly create fiat Smart dollars, as a second complementary demurrage charged currency for the United States, out of nothing, on its computers. Just as the Federal Reserve facilitates the clearing of checks on bank accounts with traditional dollars, it will similarly facilitate the clearing of electronic payments on checking accounts containing Smart dollars.

In the current single currency monetary system, the U.S. Treasury receives U.S. dollars in exchange for U.S. Treasury bonds, notes, or bills with a specified rate of interest and a specified maturity date. The amount of Treasury securities that the Federal Reserve can buy directly from the U.S. Treasury is limited by law, but the U.S. Treasury can get around this limit by selling government bonds directly to the public and to banks, which the Federal Reserve buys later during open market operations.

The U.S. Treasury will receive Smart dollars from the Federal Reserve in exchange for a new kind of Treasury security called sovereign bonds that will pay no interest, and will have no maturity date. Because a sovereign bond will have no maturity date, the holder of a sovereign bond can 'cash' a sovereign bond at any time simply by placing a sovereign bond in a demurrage checking account. Of course, the moment a sovereign bond, which does not incur demurrage, is placed in a demurrage checking account, demurrage fees will apply. Thus, although a sovereign bond will not be a debt instrument in the real sense because it will be non interest bearing, and will not pay any interest, it will nonetheless be a highly liquid financial instrument, since it can be turned into cash at any time of the holder's choice.

The extremely high liquidity of the sovereign bond will attract those investors who will prefer the liquidity and safety of a sovereign bond over the interest received from a conventional interest bearing bond with a specified maturity date. As opposed to conventional government bonds which require payment of interest at maturity, the issuance of sovereign bonds by the U.S. Treasury will not result in any interest payment on this financial instrument. Whereas a default is possible by non payment of interest on conventional interest bearing government bonds, such a default will be impossible in the case of sovereign bonds. In fact, whenever the holder of a sovereign bond will 'cash' a sovereign bond by placing it in a demurrage checking account, it will result in additional demurrage income for the U.S. Treasury.

The Federal Reserve or the U.S. Treasury can lend Smart dollars through private commercial banks, or the U.S. Treasury can spend Smart dollars into the economy in payment of its obligations. Demand for loans denominated in Smart dollars will be very strong because borrowers will prefer to take out loans in an interest free currency in which only the principal amount borrowed needs to be repaid. A loan in Smart dollars is advantageous both for the borrower and the lender. The borrower's monthly payment will be much smaller in Smart dollars than in a conventional dollar loan. The lender will not only get back the principal amount of the interest free loan, but will also receive a stream of demurrage revenue in addition.

The new demurrage currency will be in great demand because loans denominated in Smart dollars will have to be repaid in Smart dollars. In all probability, the demand for Smart dollars will outstrip the supply of Smart dollars. As an independent and freely traded convertible currency in currency exchange markets, it is a safe bet that the Smart dollar will be worth more than the traditional U.S. dollar in currency exchange markets.

Does it make sense financially for the Federal Reserve or the U.S. Treasury to provide interest free loans denominated in Smart dollars through private financial institutions? Suppose someone takes out a loan in Smart dollars to buy a residential property from a builder. The proceeds of the loan will be placed in the builder's checking account, where it will immediately incur demurrage charges. The builder will pay others, and demurrage will be imposed on their checking accounts. The act of placing the loan proceeds received in Smart dollars in the builder's checking account starts generating demurrage revenue for the U.S. Treasury. During the life of the loan, the U.S. Treasury will not only collect the monthly payments on the loan, but it will also collect the stream of demurrage payments from the principal amount of the loan, which will be circulating in Smart money checking accounts. The U.S. Treasury will not only receive demurrage income during the life of the loan, but it will continue to receive demurrage from the principal amount of the loan, for an indefinite period of time, as the principal amount of the loan continues to circulate in checking accounts throughout the economy.

How is it possible for an interest free demurrage loan to generate more revenue than a conventional interest bearing loan? The monthly payment required for a 30 year $100,000 loan at 5% simple interest would be

$536.82 per month, and the total amount collected over 30 years would be $193,256.82. For a 30 year loan of 100,000 in Smart dollars at zero percent interest, a monthly payment of only $SM 277.78 is required, which means that the borrower's monthly payment in Smart dollars will be almost half of that required in the conventional dollar loan. The lender of the Smart dollar loan will get back the entire principal amount of $SM 100,000, plus the U.S. Treasury will receive $SM 300,000 in demurrage revenue over the 30 year life of the loan. In fact, the U.S. government will keep receiving demurrage fees in the amount of $SM 10,000 every year for an indefinite period of time, because the stream of demurrage payments from the original amount of the loan will not end after 30 years.

An interest free loan in Smart dollars has the potential to produce far more revenue than a conventional interest bearing loan denominated in the current U.S. dollar. Both from the borrower's and the lender's perspective, an interest free smart loan is far superior to a conventional loan at interest. The borrower gets drastically lower monthly payments, while the U.S. Treasury keeps earning this wonderful tax on money, called demurrage, for an indefinite period of time!

In the current monetary system, bank debt money functions just like conventional money. Demand deposits are equivalent to U.S. cash currency, and so anyone can write a check on checking account money and exchange it for physical paper currency. A private bank cannot print banknotes, but it can always get cash paper currency from a Federal Reserve Bank if it runs out of cash currency. A demand deposit containing a certain amount of traditional dollars will not be automatically equivalent to the same amount of Smart dollars. It will be possible to exchange Smart dollars for conventional dollars, but only at the current market rate of exchange for the two independent currencies.

Private commercial banks will not be able to create Smart dollars, although they may continue to create traditional dollars by the fractional reserve method. Private financial institutions will be able to lend preexisting Smart dollars by obtaining Smart dollars from the Federal Reserve, but will not be able to lend Smart dollars into existence. In essence, private banks and other financial institutions will be brokers of 100% interest free, demurrage charged Smart dollars, but not creators of this complementary currency. Since the Smart dollar will be an interest free currency, banks will not be able to earn interest on Smart dollar loans, hence they will have to charge an origination fee at the time of making a Smart dollar loan in order to recover the costs of administering and servicing the loans.

The Smart dollar will differ from the conventional U.S. dollar in several important ways. First, it will be a demurrage charged currency with properties that are fundamentally different from the conventional U.S. dollar. Second, a rate of interest cannot be applied to the Smart dollar, because it will be an interest free currency. Third, it will exist only in electronic form, hence there will be no physical coin or cash paper currency associated with the Smart dollar. Fourth, it cannot be borrowed into existence, which means that Smart dollars are neither created when they are borrowed, nor are they destroyed when loans denominated in Smart dollars are repaid. Checking accounts containing Smart dollars will be accessed with smart cash cards. Just as payments are made with credit cards or debit cards in the current single currency system, in the same way, payments in Smart dollars will be made with Smart cash cards.

The German monetary and social reformer Silvio Gesell was the first person to propose a currency system based on the concept of demurrage. Gesell focused his thoughts on the structural defects inherent in the currency and monetary system, and became the first man to develop and expound the concept of demurrage by publishing his ideas on monetary reform in a series of booklets starting in 1891. When he was living in Argentina, Silvio Gesell's first work entitled, Die Reformation im Munzwesen als Brucke zum sozialen Staat (Currency Reform as a Bridge to the Social State) was published in 1891.

In the railroad industry, demurrage is the penalty that is imposed by a railroad company on a party that is responsible for the delay in loading or unloading a railroad car on time. The railroad company charges the user a fee called demurrage for each day that the railroad car sits idle on account of the fault of the party using the railroad car. When a demurrage charge is applied to a currency, it means that if the currency is not spent within the specified time frame, then a charge similar to a 'parking' fee must be paid by anyone who prefers to hold on to the money. Instead of spending the money so that it is kept in circulation, if the owner of the money chooses to hoard it, so that the money is effectively removed from circulation, then a demurrage charged currency will incur a demurrage fee which will be electronically debited to the demurrage money in a checking account. The face value of the demurrage currency will decrease by the amount of the demurrage fee which will be applied at a specific time every day of the week.

The only way to avoid a demurrage fee on a demurrage charged currency in a checking account is to spend it before the specified time each day when the fee will be automatically debited electronically. When demurrage currency is spent, the money is transferred from the buyer's demurrage checking account to the seller's demurrage checking account. A demurrage fee can be shifted from one checking account holder to another by spending it, but someone will have to pay the demurrage fee every day, on every Smart dollar, that is in circulation in checking accounts throughout the economy.

There will be no demurrage fee applied to Smart dollars placed in a demurrage savings account for a period of at least one year, and no interest will be paid on demurrage money in a demurrage savings account. It will be possible to transfer Smart dollars from a savings account to a checking account before the period of one year has been completed, but there will be a penalty for doing so. The demurrage fees that would have otherwise accumulated for the length of time that the demurrage currency was sitting in the savings account will be instantly levied, the moment money in a demurrage savings account is transferred to a checking account prematurely, before the completion of the required one year period.

The demurrage fee which is debited to the checking account of an owner of Smart dollars will be credited instantaneously to a Smart dollar checking account belonging to the United States Treasury. Monetary reform that establishes the Smart dollar must clearly state that all demurrage fees belong to the U.S. government. Although the Federal Reserve System will create the demurrage currency, it will not collect any demurrage fees generated by the demurrage currency.

The rate of demurrage will be set by the Board of Governors of the Federal Reserve System. If the rate of demurrage is set at 10%, and if there are ten trillion Smart dollars in circulation in the U.S. economy, then each year the U.S. Treasury will receive a demurrage income of one trillion Smart dollars. The U.S. Treasury can exchange this income of one trillion Smart dollars in the currency markets for traditional U.S. dollars so that it can pay any outstanding debt denominated in conventional U.S. dollars. The new demurrage charged complementary currency will be a new source of income for the United States government with which it can pay off the entire national debt denominated in traditional U.S. dollars in only a matter of a few decades. The possibility of a default on the U.S. debt by the U.S. Treasury will be removed once and for all.

The money certificates that were envisaged in the proposed Bankhead-Pettengill bill of 1933, would cease to be legal tender unless a two cent postage stamp was affixed to the dollar money certificate each week, and after 52 two cent stamps had been attached to the money certificate during the course of a year, it could be exchanged for $1 at any U.S. post office. After the money certificates were redeemed by the post office for U.S. paper currency, they would be destroyed. The money certificates proposed under the Bankhead-Pettengill bill were self liquidating, but the Smart dollar will not be self liquidating. The face value of Smart dollars in checking accounts will be reduced by 10% each year, but this will be balanced by an equivalent amount of Smart dollars in the form of demurrage fees that will collect in the coffers of the U.S. Treasury. The U.S. Treasury will spend the Smart dollars that it collects in payment of its debts and obligations, hence the amount of Smart dollars will not shrink.

In the existing single currency monetary system there is an inverse relationship between the rate of interest and investment - a higher rate of interest results in fewer investment projects. This follows from the concept of marginal efficiency of capital, which is that rate of interest which equates the price of a fixed capital asset with its present discounted value of expected income. In order for investment to occur, the marginal efficiency of capital must be higher than the rate of interest. In simpler words, the higher the rate of interest, the lower the likelihood that a specific investment project will occur. The cost of capital increases as the rate of interest on money borrowed to fund the project increases. The expected stream of income from the investment project will not be enough to pay for the cost of capital beyond a certain rate of interest.

The interest rate has a profound effect on the viability of investment projects, and the interest rate determines to a large extent the investment decisions of entrepreneurs in the U.S. economy in the current monetary system. If an interest free complementary currency were to operate side by side with the conventional interest bearing currency, investment projects that would not otherwise be viable in our conventional currency, would become possible with loans denominated in interest free Smart dollars.

The interest rate also has an enormous impact on the competitiveness of U.S. products. The cost of borrowed money is built into the price structure of goods manufactured in the United States. The availability of interest free money in the form of Smart dollars, will significantly reduce the cost of domestically manufactured products. The absence of interest on borrowed smart money will lower the prices of U.S. made goods. Prices of goods and services will be lowered not as a result of deflation, but as a consequence of lower manufacturing cost.

Deflation occurs when prices fall because the supply of goods is greater than the demand for those goods. Lack of consumer spending in the current monetary system is the main culprit responsible for deflation. Lack of spending translates into a lack of demand for goods that have already been produced, and businesses can only sell those goods by slashing the prices of those goods. If businesses are able to lower prices by cutting the cost of production through the use of improved technology, or by lowering their interest costs when they borrow money, then a lowering of prices in this manner is not harmful for the economy. But deflation caused by a lack of spending can ripple through the economy, causing unemployment, plant closings, business failures, and bankruptcies.

Sellers of goods and services are invariably inflationists since they want to get as much money as possible for their goods and services through higher prices. Buyers of goods and services are generally deflationists because they want the prices of goods and services to be as low as possible. In this respect, a demurrage charged currency favors the seller, because it forces the buyer to make a purchase before a demurrage fee is applied in his or her demurrage checking account. A demurrage currency favors the seller, and always works against deflation. A demurrage currency in a dual currency monetary system is the best safeguard against deflation caused by a lack of spending in a nation's economy.

The United States dollar exists mainly in electronic form, but it also exists as physical cash currency, which makes the application of negative interest rates impossible. If the Federal Reserve were to set a negative rate of interest to the U.S. dollar, then holders of deposits in checking or savings accounts would pull their money out and hoard their U.S. dollars as cash, because paper currency carries an interest rate of 0%. There is a cost of holding, storing, and physically safeguarding cash currency, but if the level of the negative interest rate is significant, it can become cost effective to pay for the storage of physical cash. Negative interest rates can work only with currencies that are completely electronic, and have no existence at all as physical cash. The great advantage of a completely electronic currency lies in the fact that it can have any rate of interest, positive or negative. A paper currency can only have a zero rate of interest or a positive rate of interest.

Positive interest rates do not provide an incentive for households and businesses to take out loans and engage in spending during an economic downturn. With a loan borrowed at a negative rate of interest, the face value of the loan amount remains unchanged during the duration of the loan, but a borrower pays back less money than the original amount of the loan, because he/she receives an interest payment from the lender when the loan is repaid. For this reason, negative interest loans can stimulate the economy during a recession or an economic downturn.

The ability to set a negative rate of interest is an indispensable monetary tool for a central bank with which to fight recession or deflation, but the reality of the cash paper dollar makes it rather impractical, if not altogether impossible, for the Federal Reserve to set a negative rate of interest on the U.S. dollar.

Demurrage is not the same as negative interest. A demurrage charge decreases the face value of the demurrage currency, but a negative interest charge does not decrease the face value of a currency. 100 Smart dollars held in a checking account for one year will have a face value of 90 Smart dollars if the rate of demurrage is 10% per year. If you borrow $100 in U.S. dollars from a bank at -1% interest, the bank will have to give you $1 in interest at the end of the year when it is time for you to return the $100 that the bank gave you as a loan at -1% interest. The face value of the amount borrowed remains the same, but the lender pays interest to the borrower, instead of the borrower paying interest to the lender.

As a non interest bearing currency, a positive or a negative rate of interest cannot be applied to the Smart dollar. However, if a loan in Smart dollars is made with a built in incentive of principal reduction, such that with every on time payment, the borrower gets a principal reduction of, say 1% of the remaining balance, the outcome would be similar to a negative interest loan on conventional currency. Each reduction of the principal amount of the loan, with each timely monthly payment in such a loan, would reduce the original amount of the principal needed to be repaid. Thus, although it is not possible for a Smart dollar to have any rate of interest other than a zero rate of interest, it is possible to finesse the problem of the zero bound by originating Smart dollar loans with built in principal reduction.

Central banks need to be able to use negative interest rates as a monetary tool to fight a recession or a deflation, but the reality of the present situation is that they do not have the ability to set meaningful negative interest rates. Given the framework of the current world monetary system, in which the U.S. dollar and all other major currencies of the world exist both in electronic form, and as physical paper currency, it has not been possible for major central banks of the world to set appropriate and meaningful negative interest rates. Some European central banks such as those of Sweden and Denmark have been experimenting with negative interest rates, but for the most part, the negative interest rates of these countries have been too small to be significant. For example, The Swedish Central Bank, the Riksbank, lowered its interest rate to minus 0.25 percent during the financial crisis of 2008, although this was clearly inadequate to stimulate the Swedish economy at that time.

A few ways have been suggested in recent years for removing the technological constraint of levying a carry tax on paper currency so that holders of paper money could be forced to pay a holding charge, which would then reduce their desire to hoard money. Some of these proposals to tax money include embedding a magnetic strip in each paper bill, making a currency bill ending in a certain digit cease to be legal tender, etc., but although some of these proposals are quite original in imagination, they are rather impractical.

In the current monetary system, the U.S. dollar is expected to perform several functions such as that of medium of exchange, store of value, unit of account, standard of value, and standard of deferred payment. It is a fallacy to make the assumption that this one kind of money can effectively play all of these five roles simultaneously, because some of these roles contradict each other. For example, the conventional dollar cannot function as an efficient medium of exchange and at the same time serve as a convenient store of value. For the purpose of serving as a store of value, money must be hoarded, but the act of hoarding money removes it from circulation until its owner decides to spend it or lend it. When money is hoarded, it ceases to function as a medium of exchange for the time period of its hoarding.

These two roles of money are clearly in contradiction to each other because, whereas a medium of exchange functions optimally when it circulates, a store of value requires its removal from circulation, or at least a temporary withdrawal from circulation. Money can be hoarded by its owners without any physical deterioration or cost of storage, but goods and merchandise are subject to spoilage, decay, and deterioration, and consequently perishable over time. For this reason, the suppliers of goods and services, and providers of labor, are always under pressure to sell their goods, or provide their services, as quickly as possible, but holders of money can afford to wait as they are under no such compulsion.

Whenever money is hoarded, circulation of the money that is being hoarded is interrupted, and exchanges of goods and services that would have been otherwise possible with this money are prevented form taking place. Money that is withheld from circulation and kept idle leads to a loss in economic activity that is directly proportional to time. The moment a sum of money is hoarded, it loses its function as a medium of exchange, and switches to its other role as a store of value. The possibility that money can be immobilized by hoarding constitutes a fatal flaw in the currency system currently in operation in the United States.

The conventional U.S. dollar is the world's reserve currency, and for the purpose of serving as the world's reserve currency, it is necessary for the United States to run current account deficits so that it can supply the rest of the world with U.S. dollars. The role of the U.S. dollar as the world's reserve currency, is making the United States more and more indebted to foreigners, and at the same time the United States is becoming unsustainably burdened with debt. The U.S. dollar's future as the world's reserve currency is in doubt because of this unsustainable debt burden. A new demurrage charged complementary currency can produce an additional stream of income, other than taxes, to ease the burden of this unsustainable debt. The possibility of a collapse in the value of the U.S. dollar in international currency markets can be averted if this unsustainable burden of debt is eased with revenue from the new complementary currency. The role of the U.S. dollar as the world's reserve currency can continue uninterrupted, if the U.S. monetary system is reformed to embrace the concept of a dual currency system.

The grave problem of budget and trade deficits requires imaginative thinking and an unconventional approach to a conventional problem. We cannot tackle the problems caused by our massive and bourgeoning debt with the use of outdated and ineffective monetary tools that we currently have in our possession. We need a modern and conceptually different kind of money to address our massive debt problem. We cannot take the wholesale risk of completely replacing our current monetary system with an untried, untested, and unknown monetary system. But we can, and must make incremental changes to our current monetary system. The introduction of the Smart dollar as a second currency, within a new dual currency system, is urgently needed to modernize the current monetary system of the United States.

This book is organized in three parts. The first part is a summary of the important events in the political and financial history of the United States. The second part is a summary of how the monetary system of the United States has evolved over the years until the establishment of the Federal Reserve System. The third part of this book explains how a national demurrage charged currency can help the U.S. avert the impending disaster of a default on the national debt.

# THE REVOLUTIONARY WAR

After years of unrest, sometimes punctuated with violence, America's war for independence from Britain began on April 19, 1775 with the battles of Lexington and Concord. The militia that fought the British included many African Americans, both free and enslaved. The members of this militia were really loyal British subjects who were ready to fight for their rights. These loyal British subjects were against injustice and oppression and could not allow insolent British forces to trample over their legitimate rights. They were not American citizens yet because the declaration of independence would come later on July 4, 1776.

In spite of the overwhelming superiority of the British in arms and numbers, the revolutionary patriots fought tenaciously, and courageously; confronted by a ruthless and merciless enemy, they refused to be cowed into submission. At the end of the day, on April 19, 1775 the British occupation forces would find out that they had vastly underestimated the tenacity, resolve, courage, and determination of this small band of valiant fighters. On April 19, 1775 a rag tag band of revolutionary patriots humiliated an Imperial British force which lost 73 killed and many more wounded whereas the revolutionary militia lost 49 killed in action.

The turning point of the revolutionary war came in the fall of 1781 when the siege known as the battle of Yorktown began on September 28, 1781. Yorktown, named after the city of York in Yorkshire, England was founded as a port in 1691 by English colonists to export tobacco to Europe. Located on the York river at the mouth of Chesapeake Bay in Virginia, Yorktown had a population of about 2000 people in 1750 and was the base of British general Lord Charles Cornwallis. Lord Cornwallis, commander of British occupation forces in the Southern theatre of operations during the American revolutionary war, had retreated to the Yorktown peninsula in June 1781 to rest and reequip his battered forces.

At this time an allied force of French and American forces were positioned north of New York City when news arrived that the thirty-four ship French battle fleet, with three thousand soldiers, commanded by Francois Count de Grasse, had departed the French colony of St. Domingue (which is now Haiti), and was heading towards Chesapeake Bay in Virginia. General George Washington, commander of the American Revolutionary Army, ordered an American force of 5,000 troops to cut off any possible retreat of Cornwallis and his forces by land from Yorktown, while the French naval fleet blocked any escape of British forces from Yorktown by sea. Thus, Cornwallis and his army were trapped in Yorktown by the combined allied forces of French and American soldiers.

Cornwallis and his army were bombarded incessantly night and day for three straight weeks until Cornwallis finally agreed to surrender to General George Washington on October 17, 1781. Cornwallis declined to attend the formal surrender ceremony on October 19, 1781 with the excuse that he was ill. He ordered his second in command, General Charles O'Hara to carry his sword to the victorious allied French and American commanders. This allied French and American victory at Yorktown was decisive in determining the outcome of the American war of independence from the British and was instrumental in ending the revolutionary war.

In 1775 the thirteen rebellious colonies with a population of 2.5 million, including about half a million slaves, were fighting Great Britain - an imperial power of 8 million inhabitants. The fight for independence would continue until Great Britain would finally agree to accept and recognize the United States as a sovereign and independent nation by signing the Treaty of Paris on September 3, 1783.

# FINANCING THE REVOLUTIONARY WAR

A fledgling confederation of thirteen rebellious states was engaged in hostilities that lasted seven years against an implacable enemy with no moral compunctions; an enemy which ruled a vast empire of colonies over which the sun could never set. Imperial Great Britain had enormous wealth, huge amounts of tax revenue from its subjects, an awesome military capability, and excellent credit rating in world credit markets. How was it possible for this upstart confederation of thirteen American colonies to pay for its revolutionary war against such a formidable imperial power whose tentacles reached every corner of the world?

Actually, it was not easy for the Continental Congress that served as the government of these thirteen rebellious colonies from 1974 to 1789 to come up with the money to finance this war of independence from Great Britain. In retaliation for acts of colonial defiance, the British parliament passed the Coercive Act in 1774 which consisted of several harsh laws that the colonists were required to obey. In response to these Coercive Act laws, 56 delegates appointed by 12 colonies (all colonies except for Georgia) met in secret at Carpenters Hall in Philadelphia for the First Continental Congress from September 5 to October 26, 1774.

The 56 delegates drafted a declaration of rights and grievances which demanded the repeal of thirteen acts of the British parliament which had been enacted since 1763. Benjamin Franklin presented the colonists' demands in person to the British parliament, but King George III refused to accede to these demands. Instead, the British government opted for a military solution to the crisis, and Boston was occupied by British troops.

The first shots of the revolutionary war were fired on April 19, 1775 in Lexington and Concord, and three weeks later, the Second Continental Congress was convened in Philadelphia on May 10, 1775. Congress decided to organize armed resistance to British authority by voting to create a Continental army with Congressman George Washington of Virginia as the Commanding General of this Continental army. Congress authorized the establishment of a new paper currency called the Continental to pay for the expenses of maintaining this army and to finance the purchases of arms and ammunition required by this army. On July 4, 1776 Congress declared independence from Great Britain.

The Continental Congress adopted the Articles of Confederation on November 15, 1777. This was the first constitution of the United States and it created a loose confederation of sovereign states with a weak central government. According to the Articles of Confederation, Congress could declare war and manage foreign affairs but it neither had the power to tax nor the power to regulate commerce within the confederation. Without the power to impose or collect taxes during this period, Congress had to ask the thirteen confederate states to provide money, material, arms, ammunition, supplies and soldiers for the war effort. Without a tax system in place to provide a stream of revenue, and dependent on the thirteen states to provide voluntary payments to Congress, it became difficult for Congress to finance the war effort. Ratification of the Articles of Confederation by all thirteen states did not occur until March 1, 1781.

Some confederate states were not making the necessary voluntary payments to Congress and several states were issuing their own separate currencies. As a result, the continental currency introduced by Congress had to compete with several different currencies circulating within the confederation. The continental dollar also had to face financial terrorism from the infamous British Empire. In order to destroy the value of the continental dollar, the British launched a covert operation to introduce counterfeit continental dollars within the confederation. These counterfeit dollars were printed and then distributed throughout the territory of the thirteen confederate states by British occupation forces and their agents loyal to the British Crown. The Continental dollar depreciated quickly as a consequence of this rapid expansion in the supply of Continental dollars. 168 paper Continental dollars were needed in exchange for one dollar in specie in 1771. The Continental dollar had collapsed and was almost worthless. The expression 'not worth a continental' is a reflection of this collapse in the value of the Continental dollar.

In his book 'A History of Money and Banking in the United States', (page 59), the late Professor Murray N. Rothbard wrote:

"The total money supply of the United States at the beginning of the Revolution has been estimated at $12 million. Congress launched its first paper issue of $2 million in late June 1775, and before the notes were printed it had already concluded that another $1 million was needed. Before the end of the year, a full $6 million in paper issues was issued or authorized, a dramatic increase of 50 percent in the money supply in one year.

The issue of this fiat "Continental" paper rapidly escalated over the next few years. Congress issued $6 million in 1775, $19 million in 1776, $13 million in 1777, $64 million in 1778, and $125 million in 1779. This was a total issue of over $225 million in five years superimposed upon a pre-existing money supply of $12 million. The result was, as could be expected, a rapid price inflation in terms of the paper notes, and a corollary accelerating depreciation of the paper in terms of specie. Thus, at the end of 1776, the Continentals were worth $1 to $1.25 in specie; by the fall of the following year, its value had fallen to 3-to-1; by December 1778 the value was 6.8-to-1; and by December 1779, to the negligible 42-to-1. By the spring of 1781, the Continentals were virtually worthless, exchanging on the market at 168 paper dollars to one dollar in specie. This collapse of the Continental currency gave rise to the phrase, 'not worth a Continental'".

When Robert Morris, a Congressman from Philadelphia, was appointed Superintendent of Finance in February, 1781, Continental currency was not being issued any more. The government of the Confederate union was in dire financial straits and Congress requested Morris to help save the Confederate Union's tottering finances. Robert Morris presented a plan which created the Confederate union's first national and private commercial bank, as well as a de facto central bank. The Bank of North America received a charter on May 26, 1781 from both the Continental

Congress and the State of Pennsylvania, and opened its doors for business on January 7, 1782.

The Bank of England which was established in 1694, was the model for the organization of the new Bank of North America. In essence it was designed to practice fractional reserve banking by issuing paper currency backed by reserves of specie. It was granted a monopoly license to issue paper currency and its banknotes could be used to pay all taxes and duties owed to states and the Confederate union government. The banknotes of the Bank of North America could be nominally redeemed in specie, yet these banknotes continued to decline in value outside the Philadelphia area because of the market's lack of confidence in the bank. The Confederate union's stock in the Bank of North America, which was more than half of the bank's capital, was sold to private investors, and towards the end of 1783, the Confederate union's debt to the Bank of North America had been repaid.

On September 3, 1783 the Treaty of Paris was signed in Paris by representatives of King George III of Great Britain and representatives of the United States of America. At the time Congress ratified the Treaty of Paris on January 14, 1784, the account of the United States at the Bank of America was closed and Robert Morris had relinquished his position as the Superintendent of the US Treasury. After operating for approximately three years and eight months, Bank of North America's charter was repealed by the Pennsylvania legislature on September 13, 1785. The Bank of North America was granted a new charter by the Pennsylvania legislature on March 17, 1787, but this time under greater restrictive conditions, which made it practically impossible for the Bank of North America to function as a central bank. This effectively ended the Confederate union's experiment with a central bank.

During the revolutionary war the rebellious colonies received loans from a number of European countries including France, Spain and the Netherlands. After the battles of Lexington and Concord in April of 1775, the French Government began to ship war material in secret to the revolutionary militias to help them in their fight against the British. By the end of the revolutionary war the French had provided loans in the amount of two million dollars to the Americans. The cost of the revolutionary war was 165 million pounds sterling in 1783. Although the American

Confederation was assisted by the French with money and military assistance, the war was paid for primarily by Americans themselves. 39% of the money for the war effort came from the 13 states printing their own money, 28% came from the Continental Congress printing its own money, 14% was provided by debt certificates issued by the 13 states, 10% was provided by loan certificates issued by the Continental Congress, 6% of the money needed for the war were received as loans from Europe, and 3% was generated by bond sales to wealthy, patriotic Americans by Congress.

# AFTER THE REVOLUTIONARY WAR

The United States Constitution was signed on September 17, 1787 by delegates to the Constitutional Convention, presided over by George Washington, in the Assembly Room of the Pennsylvania State House, now known as Independence Hall, in Philadelphia, Pennsylvania. The United States Constitution, the Supreme Law of the United States of America, came into effect on March 4, 1789, and it replaced the Articles of Confederation adopted by the Continental Congress in 1777. Congress specified March 4, 1789 as the date when a new government under this Constitution would begin to operate.

Article 1, Section 8 of the US Constitution gives Congress the power to lay and collect taxes, duties, imposts, and excises, to pay the debts and provide for the common defense and general welfare of the United States; it also gives Congress the power to borrow money on the credit of the United States, to regulate commerce with foreign nations, among the several states, and the Indian tribes; it gives Congress the power to establish a uniform rule of naturalization, and uniform laws on the subject of bankruptcies throughout the United States; it gives Congress the power to coin money, regulate the value thereof, and of foreign coin, and for the standard of weights and measures; and other powers in addition to these.

Article 1, Section 8 of the Constitution permits Congress to coin money and to regulate its value whereas Section 10 denies the states the right to coin or to print their own money. The Constitution does not explicitly state that Congress has the authority to issue paper money; however, it does not deny Congress the authority to issue paper money either. Similarly, the Constitution does not explicitly grant Congress the power to establish a national bank, but it does not say that Congress has no power to incorporate a national bank. Although the Constitution is silent on banking, it can be argued that because Congress has the power to tax, to borrow money, and to regulate interstate and foreign commerce, Congress therefore also has the power to enact any law that is required to execute powers explicitly granted to it by the Constitution.

If the words of the Constitution are to be interpreted literally, then the U.S. money supply must consist only of gold and silver coins minted by the U.S. Treasury and any foreign coin acceptable to Congress. In 1787 the quantity of gold and silver that the U.S. had in its possession were insufficient to fund an adequate money supply. At that time the U.S. had no substantial gold and silver mines, and the U.S. was consistently running trade deficits with other nations. This meant that the U.S. could neither produce substantial amounts of gold and silver from indigenous mining operations to augment its stocks of gold and silver, nor could it purchase gold from abroad with money earned from trade surpluses. Thus, there was no practical way to increase the money supply of a nation whose monetary system was based purely on gold and silver.

The militia of the thirteen Confederate states had inflicted a humiliating defeat on the mighty armed forces of an arrogant imperial power which had been finally compelled to acknowledge America's independence. However, in 1787 the young nation was facing serious economic problems. Years of warfare had disrupted trade and commerce and had ruined the economy of the fledgling nation. The United States as a nation was mired in debt, most of its people were driven into poverty by the protracted conflict, many of its citizens were either deep in debt or bankrupt, the Continental dollar which was printed indiscriminately to finance the revolutionary war was almost worthless, and inflation was rampant. In these circumstances there was the frightening possibility that the unity of the young nation might fracture and disintegrate.

Acting under the powers granted to Congress by the U.S. Constitution that was ratified on March 4, 1789, Congress passed the Tariff Act of 1789 which was signed into law on July 4, 1789. President George Washington appointed Alexander Hamilton as the Secretary of the Treasury after the Treasury Department was created by an act of Congress in September

1789. In response to a request from Congress that Hamilton submit an economic plan to address the economic problems of the new country, Hamilton prepared several reports which included The Report on Public Credit dated January 9, 1790, The Report on the Bank dated December 13, 1790, the Report on the Subject of a Mint dated January 28, 1791, and the Report on Manufactures dated December 5, 1791.

Alexander Hamilton's first Report on the Public credit was a 40,000 word document that analyzed the financial position of the United States. According to this report, the national debt inherited from the Continental Congress was in the amount of about $77 million, of which $40 million was in domestic debt, $12 million was in foreign debt, and $25 million was the total debt of all thirteen states.

Hamilton's report suggested that Congress should honor both federal and state debt in its entirety. The report called for full payment at face value to holders of government securities, and also recommended that the federal government accept the responsibility for the funding of all outstanding state debt. In order to pay the interest and the principal on this debt, and to generate revenue needed to defray the expenses of running the central government, Hamilton proposed the imposition of a new tariff and the issuance of new debt at lower interest rates to retire the older debt.

Alexander Hamilton's plan called for the central government to assume liability for the combined debt of the federal government and the states, but states such as Maryland, Pennsylvania, North Carolina, and Virginia that had paid off their debts were not happy that they should be burdened with taxes to pay the debts of other states like Massachusetts and South Carolina. This issue was hotly debated for several months in Congress. Northern states which were more industrialized than southern states preferred high tariffs to protect their industry from competition, whereas southern states favored low tariffs so that imported products would be cheaper. In order to win the support of recalcitrant states for Hamilton's debt plan, James Madison and Thomas Jefferson engineered a deal: the national capital of the nation would be relocated to a site along the Potomac river - the river that forms the boundary between the two southern states of Maryland and Virginia.

In the end, Hamilton's debt plan proved to be quite successful mainly because his debt plan explicitly acknowledged America's debts, and showed that the young nation intended to repay its debts in full. This commitment to honor its financial obligations on the part of the United States attracted European investors who pumped increasing amounts of capital into the new country.

After the passage of the Tariff Act in 1789, Hamilton delivered his second report entitled, "The Second Report on the Further Provision Necessary For Establishing Public Credit" (Report on a National Bank) on December 13, 1790 in which he proposed the creation of a privately held but publicly financed national bank. This proposed bank would be similar to the Bank of England which was established in 1694, but would differ from it in some significant ways. The Bank of England was nationalized in 1946, but in 1790 it was 100% privately owned whereas the proposed U.S. national bank would be 20% owned by the U.S. Government. The proposed U.S. bank would practice fractional reserve banking by holding a specified amount of specie in reserve as a ratio of its loans whereas the Bank of England was not bound by such a requirement. Unlike the Bank of England where each shareholder had one vote, the number of votes that a shareholder of the national bank would possess would depend upon the size of the shareholder's investment. The national bank would be enjoined from trading in commodities and would not be able to make loans to state or local governments without government approval.

Hamilton delineated several important functions that a national bank could perform. It could generate a money supply that was a multiple of the required reserve ratio, that is, the banknote to specie ratio, and thereby produce a money supply which was commensurate with the needs of the country's economy. The paper currency that it would issue would in effect be a national currency because its banknotes would have nationwide acceptance, and could be used to pay taxes to the government. It could act as a private commercial bank and offer banking facilities for commercial transactions. It could make loans to the public as well as to the government if the government needed loans. Finally, it could serve as a safe depository for holding private and government funds.

The proposed bank would have a twenty year charter starting in 1791, and ending in 1811, at which time Congress could either renew the bank's charter or let the charter expire. During the twenty year term of this bank, Congress would not be able to charter another national bank, although the states could authorize additional intrastate banks. Foreign investors, regardless of whether they lived abroad or resided in the United States, would be permitted to purchase stock and become stockholders of this bank, but would not have the right to vote.

Hamilton's proposed bank met with fierce resistance from Southern members of Congress who argued that the primary beneficiary of such a bank would be the industrial North to the detriment of the agricultural South. Secretary of State Thomas Jefferson and Representative from Virginia James Madison, who were at the forefront of the opposition to the national bank, both believed that the creation of such an institution was a violation of the Constitution. James Madison also had reservations regarding the twenty year term of the bank's charter because he felt that the new country would be taking an enormous risk by granting such a long charter of twenty years to an unknown and untested entity. Attorney General Edmund Randolph was also of the opinion that Congress was not authorized by the Constitution to create a national bank. This was the first time that the new United States government had to face a Constitutional issue.

# THE FIRST BANK OF THE UNITED STATES

Both Edmund Randolph and Thomas Jefferson advised the President to exercise his veto, and so on February 16, 1791 President George Washington forwarded the comments of Edmund Randolph and Thomas Jefferson in writing to Alexander Hamilton, asking him for a rejoinder on this matter within one week. Hamilton's refutation of Randolph's and Jefferson's arguments against the creation of a national bank was simply brilliant. Hamilton contended that although it was true that the Constitution did not say that the authority to Congress was available for creating a national bank, yet at the same time it was also true that the Constitution did not say that such authority to Congress was unavailable.

After receiving Hamilton's lengthy refutation of the arguments against the proposed bank, President George Washington signed the bill for the establishment of the new bank on February 25, 1791. The bill that created the bank specified that the First Bank of the United States could charge a maximum interest rate of six percent on its loans. Thomas Willing who was previously President of the Bank of North America, Mayor of Philadelphia, Secretary to the Congress of delegates at Albany, and a Judge of the Supreme Court of Pennsylvania, became the President of the new bank. He remained as the president of the bank until 1807.

In a resolution dated March 3, 1791 Congress authorized the formation of a mint, and the U.S. Mint was established on April 2, 1792 in Philadelphia. President George Washington appointed David Rittenhouse as the 1$^{st}$ Director of the Mint at an annual salary of $2,000. In 1799 the U.S. Mint became an independent agency reporting directly to the President.

President George Washington appointed three commissioners on March 19, 1791 for taking subscriptions for the new bank: Thomas Willing, David Rittenhouse, and Samuel Howell. Bank subscriptions or "scrips", which cost $25 each payable in gold or silver, were first offered for sale in July 1791 and were soon sold out. A scrip was actually a down payment on a First Bank of America stock which had a price of $400 per share.

The First Bank of the United States started operating in Philadelphia on December 12, 1791 with an initial capitalization of ten million dollars of which the U.S. government owned two million dollars, and the rest, eight million dollars belonged to private investors, both domestic and foreign. Ten million dollars was an enormous sum of money in 1791 which meant that because of this large capitalization, the First Bank of the United States was the biggest institution of any kind at that time in America. Despite the fact that it was the largest shareholder of the bank, the U.S. government did not directly manage or otherwise control the bank, but the Treasury Secretary had the right to inspect the bank's books and ask for a statement of the bank's financial condition as often as once every week. As a shareholder, the U.S. government did receive a share of the bank's profits.

The board of directors of the bank, selected by stockholders at a meeting of stockholders in 1791, consisted of 25 members who included lawyers, merchants, brokers, and also some senators and congressmen. Four branches of the bank were opened in Baltimore, Boston, Charleston, and New York in 1792, and subsequently four additional branches were opened in Norfolk, Washington, Savannah, and New Orleans. The existence of so many branches enabled the bank to circulate its banknotes much more efficiently than a state bank, and the location of all these branches at port cities facilitated the collection of the government's tax revenues, much of which came from customs duties and tariffs. Through this network of branches, the bank was able to move the governments deposits and pay the government's bills throughout the country.

In addition to serving the needs of the government, the First Bank of the United States also served as a commercial bank for the public by accepting deposits and making loans to private citizens and businesses.

It was able to issue paper currency and create checking account money by making loans to individuals and businesses. Whereas state banknotes suffered from lack of wide acceptance and could not be used to pay taxes, the currency issued by the Bank of the United States could be used to pay taxes and was generally readily accepted all over the country. It was the largest bank with branches throughout the country and consequently issued more banknotes and made more loans than any state bank. Since its inception in 1791 the Bank of the United States continued to loan so much money to the U.S. government that by the close of 1795 it had extended more than $6 million in loans - more than half of its capital - to the government, and the directors of the bank requested the government for partial repayment of the outstanding loan balance. The government's financial position and credit were rather weak in 1795 and so instead of trying to borrow more money in the credit markets to pay down its debt to the bank, the Treasury repaid the bank by selling its shares of stock in the bank.

Although there were 117 state banks in 1811 which were issuing their own banknotes, the Bank of the United States had about $5 million of its currency in circulation which constituted about twenty percent of the U.S. money supply at that time. Its paper currency was the equivalent of a national currency in those days. With a 40% specie to banknote ratio in 1809, the Bank of the United States was the most liquid bank in the U.S. and at the same time profitable, making most of its money by extending loans to the government and the public. In the words of Treasury Secretary Albert Gallatin, the bank was "wisely and skillfully managed".

The bank's charter came up for renewal in 1811, but the very success of the Bank of the United States was responsible for its demise because state banks were simply not able to compete with this bank. Supporters of state banks were the most vocal critics of the national bank. The currency of the Bank of America was not discounted, but the currency issued by state banks were generally discounted. In other words when the holder of a state banknote made a purchase with the state banknote, the banknote was discounted, that is, the holder of the banknote received only a fraction of the nominal face value of the banknote as payment in the form of goods and services, or in exchange for gold or silver.

In 1811 foreigners who owned approximately 70% of the bank's stock were not allowed to vote, but they were entitled to receive the dividend of 8.4% on the shares that they owned. Opponents of the bank argued that if another twenty year charter was granted to the bank, it would lead to the transfer of approximately $12 million in gold and silver to foreign stockholders of the bank. This was another factor that sealed the bank's fate. Critics of the bank pointed to this fact and asserted that the United States had limited stocks of specie and as such could not afford to repatriate its scarce supply of gold and silver to investors overseas.

The Democrats, many of whom were adamantly opposed to the continued operation of the Bank of the United States, were in a majority in 1811 and looked forward to ending the bank's charter. Two prominent Democrats, President James Madison and Treasury Secretary Albert Gallatin, crossed party lines to support the renewal of the bank's charter, but the bill to renew the bank's charter was defeated by a single vote in the House on February 20, 1811. The Senate was deadlocked on February 20, 1811 when Vice President George Clinton broke the tie by casting a negative vote. Thus, the Bank of the United States was shut down on March 3, 1811 and became a part of history.

# THE WAR OF 1812 WITH GREAT BRITAIN

In 1812 Great Britain still retained the western forts that it had agreed to return to the U.S. when it signed the treaty of Paris in 1783 to end the revolutionary war. On the high seas Great Britain was engaged in a policy of "impressment" of U.S. sailors which in practice meant that the British were intercepting and boarding U.S. vessels to forcibly remove U.S. sailors in order to impress them into service in the British navy. In the western frontier region Great Britain was supporting and arming Native Americans who were attacking American settlers, and with the intention of restricting trade between France and the United states, Great Britain announced a number of rules that the U.S. needed to obey. The U.S. found it impossible to stomach this outrageous behavior from the British, and in response to calls for the U.S. to act in self defense, President James Madison signed a declaration of war against Great Britain on June 18, 1812. Both the U.S. House and the Senate were bitterly divided on war with Britain, but in the end Congress voted for the war.

In the first military campaign of the war, U.S. forces led by William Hull launched an invasion of Canada by crossing into Canada from Detroit. Hull's forces were badly mauled and his attack completely repulsed. British forces commanded by Brock and Tecumseh then marched across the U.S. border and captured Detroit without firing a single shot on August 16, 1812. The conquest of Canada was not going to be as easy as Thomas Jefferson had once famously described in the following words:

"The acquisition of Canada, as far as the neighborhood of Quebec, will be a mere matter of marching, and will give us experience for the attack of Halifax the next, and the final expulsion of England from the American continent."

A second unsuccessful invasion of Canada was launched by U.S. forces led by Stephen Van Rensselaer who was in command of a contingent of 3,100 troops. Rensselaer sent a part of this force across the Niagara river to attack Queenstown, but Rensselaer's advance force was encircled by British forces and had no choice but to surrender. In the ensuing battle British commander Isaac Brock was killed in action on October 13, 1812, but 925 Americans were captured and taken into captivity as prisoners of war.

After two more years of fighting during which both sides won and lost battles, British forces led by Major General Robert Ross overran U.S. militia stationed at Blandenburg in Maryland, and then marched another five miles unopposed, to capture the U.S. capital of Washington D.C. on August 24, 1814. On this day, when a detachment of British troops arrived at about 8 PM in the evening at the Executive Mansion, now known as the White House, they found an elegant dinner ready for about forty guests in the dining room. After finishing a sumptuous dinner in the dining room of the White House that evening, the victorious British forces then burned the White House. The U.S. Capitol which contained the 3,000 volume collection of the Library of Congress at that time, was also torched as was many other government buildings. The house belonging to Treasury Secretary Albert Gallatin was razed to the ground.

After occupying Washington for only 24 hours, the British withdrew their troops from the city; it was a strategic withdrawal because the British reckoned that their forces in Washington DC were not sufficient to withstand an American counterattack to retake their capital. Thereafter, Great Britain lost several major battles and the tide of the war began to turn in America's favor. The turning point of the war came after a naval force commanded by Thomas MacDonough was victorious in the battle of Plattsburg on September 11, 1814. This loss forced Sir George Prevost, in charge of a large British force, to scuttle his planned invasion of the U.S. northeast and instead compelled him to withdraw his forces to Canada. A few months later, to end the war of 1812, Great Britain and the U.S.

signed the Treaty of Ghent in Belgium on December 24, 1814 and so after 32 months of armed conflict, the war of 1812 came to a final conclusion.

Unaware of the Treaty of Ghent, because news traveled slowly across the Atlantic in those days, a large British force launched a desperate frontal assault on the city of New Orleans on January 8, 1815. Defending New Orleans was a mixed force of militiamen, slaves, native Americans and pirates. The French pirate Jean Lafitte and his comrades, in return for a legal pardon, had agreed to help future President Andrew Jackson. This allied force of Jean Lafitte and Andrew Jackson, under the command of Andrew Jackson, blunted and repulsed the British offensive. The battle of New Orleans culminated in a stunning and spectacular victory for the U.S. in what would be the final military engagement of the war of 1812.

# THE SECOND BANK OF THE UNITED STATES

The U.S. went to war in 1812 without any preparation for the funding of the upcoming war with Great Britain. There was no federal income tax in 1812. The federal government's revenues came primarily from customs duties and land sales, but as soon as the war started, these two sources of income declined precipitously because of the suspension of trade with Britain and France. To increase its income from tariffs, Congress raised custom duties by as much as 100%, but in spite of this, income from tariffs actually fell because the overall volume of imports and exports declined significantly as the war progressed. Exports declined from $61 million in 1811 to only $7 million in 1814, and imports fell from $53 million in 1811 to $13 million in 1814. Lack of foreign trade severely affected other sectors of the economy such as shipbuilding and agriculture, and the drastic decline in imports caused the prices of imported items to soar by an average of 70%. Secretary of State Albert Gallatin imposed taxes on whiskey, salt, land and slaves. The direct tax on land and property was primarily on real estate. State governments were given 15% of the proceeds of this property tax for appraising, collecting, and remitting the property taxes to the federal government. This federal property tax was terminated in 1815.

In the absence of a national central bank which could provide loans and credit, the U.S. government now had to depend primarily on state chartered banks to buy its bonds so that it could finance the ongoing war with Great Britain. In 1811 there were 117 state banks with $14.9

million in specie and $42.2 million in banknotes and demand deposits. In 1815 there were 212 banks with 13.5 million in specie and $79 million in banknotes and demand deposits. During this period from 1811 to 1815 the stocks of specie held by banks had decreased, but the amount of paper currency and demand deposits had almost doubled. This twofold expansion in the money supply caused price inflation that averaged 28% to 35% in various parts of the country from 1811 to 1814. The reserve ratio of banks deteriorated from 35% to 17% and the financial position of many banks became precarious.

A run on banks in Washington and Baltimore was precipitated by the British invasion of the Chesapeake in August 1814, forcing them to halt payments to their customers in gold and silver. Very soon Southern, Western, and middle Atlantic state banks also began to refuse specie payments, and in this way many insolvent banks avoided certain liquidation and closure. The U.S. government allowed banks to suspend specie payments from August 1814 to February 1817, a little over two years after the war of 1812 ended.

To finance the war of 1812, the U.S. government sold short term Treasury notes and long term Treasury bonds mainly to banks located in Southern, Western, and Mid-Atlantic states, and received banknotes from these banks in exchange for the federal securities. State banks in the New England region (the states of Connecticut, Delaware, Maine, Massachusetts, New Hampshire, Rhode Island, and Vermont) happened to be more conservative and prudent than state banks in other parts of the country, and were willing to buy very little federal government debt. The reluctance of New England banks to purchase U.S. debt was a reflection of the fact that the people of New England were not very enthusiastic about the war of 1812, and in fact had even threatened to secede from the United States. The U.S. government used the banknotes that it received from banks outside the New England region to purchase arms, ammunition, and other products manufactured in New England. In other words, the U.S. government was paying for goods produced in the New England states with paper currency issued by states outside the New England region.

The companies in New England that received these banknotes as payment from the federal government then deposited these banknotes in banks in their area. Lacking confidence in the banknotes that it was getting from state banks outside their region, New England banks asked for redemption of those banknotes in specie. Those banks of course, did not have the specie to redeem their banknotes, and were only saved because the government allowed them to suspend specie payments.

Before declaring war on Britain, Congress took the important step of boosting the strength of its armed forces to a total of 10,000 men, but it had not taken any steps to prepare itself financially for the future war. $10 million was necessary to meet the expenses of the war in 1812, but the government only had money to pay for its regular expenses. The money for military expenditures had to be borrowed, and so Congress approved a loan of $11 million and higher customs duties to pay for the war during 1812. In 1813 Congress again authorized a total of $28.5 million in loans for the war effort. In April of 1813, financiers John Jacob Aster, David Parish, and Stephen Girard, after being persuaded in a meeting with Treasury Secretary Albert Gallatin, agreed to purchase $9 million worth of government securities. During the course of the next three years, these three financiers would become intimately involved with Jacob Barker, future Treasury Secretary Alexander Dallas, and Representative John C. Calhoun of South Carolina in the formation of the Second Bank of the United States in 1816. These six men held the firm conviction that only the creation of a national bank could lift the nation out of its financial doldrums. They felt that a national bank could help the U.S. government issue debt to pay for the war, stabilize the currency, curb runaway inflation, and improve the U.S. government's credit. In February of 1814 Representative John C. Calhoun presented a plan to establish a national bank with its headquarters in the District of Columbia, but the bill did not pass.

William Jones replaced Albert Gallatin as Treasury Secretary at the end of 1813, and in his report of January 1814, Jones anticipated a shortage of about $30 million for the year 1814. The U.S. needed new loans and taxes for military expenditures and for servicing debt that would mature and become due in 1814. However, it was becoming more and more difficult to find buyers of the government's debt; investors began to doubt the solvency of the government. The full faith and credit of the United States government was at stake. The government's revenues were simply insufficient to pay the cost of the ongoing war and simultaneously to service debt that was maturing and becoming due in 1814. The United States did not have the money to service its debt obligations, and so the United States defaulted on debt that matured in 1814. The United States government was indeed bankrupt in November of 1814.

According to author Donald R. Hickey, in his book, The War of 1812: A Forgotten Conflict (page 233): "Once the banks went off a a specie-paying basis, they stopped honoring each other's notes. As a result, the administration could no longer transfer funds from one part of the country to another. Although government surpluses accumulated in some banks in the middle and southern states, federal funds were quickly exhausted in Boston, New York, and Philadelphia, where most of the interest on the national debt was due. The suspension of specie payments hurt the government in another way. Bank paper circulated at a 15-30 percent discount and yet the Treasury accepted it at par for taxes and loans. With only depreciated bank notes and treasury notes coming into the Treasury, the government had no currency that could readily be used to meet its obligations. For all practical purposes, public credit was extinct and the government was bankrupt."

The financial and economic condition of the United States in November of 1814 resembled its plight after the revolutionary war. The country's credit was in tatters, its debt had increased, prices of everything had soared, and rampant inflation had reduced the purchasing power of its money to only a fraction of what it was before the start of the war. According to the Bureau of the Public Debt, "Total public debt increased from $45.2 million on January 1812 to $119.2 million as of September 30, 1815. The government could not even pay its armed forces on time; the U.S. was several months behind in its payment of salaries to its soldiers. The Springfield Armory which supplied weapons to the armed forces was shuttered, and new recruits for the army was down to a trickle. In these circumstances, would it be possible for the United States to continue the war with Great Britain?

Lady luck provided a reprieve for the United States. Fortunately for the U.S., the war would end within a month after the government's default on its debt. In August of 1814 negotiations for peace had started in Ghent, Belgium. Representatives from Britain and the United States finalized an agreement to end the conflict, and the Treaty of Ghent was signed in

Ghent on December 24, 1814. The total cost of the war of 1812 was $158 million out of which $90 million was spent on the army and navy. The interest alone on the money borrowed to fight the war was $16 million.

After he became Treasury Secretary in the fall of 1814, Alexander Dallas outlined a plan for creating a national bank. In early 1815 a bill to create a national bank passed both the House and the Senate, but was vetoed by President James Madison. News of the peace treaty with England led to the postponement of another bank bill for a whole year. In January of 1816, President James Madison again vetoed another bank bill that had cleared both chambers of Congress. Finally on April 10, 1816 President Madison signed a bank bill into law authorizing the establishment of a national bank for a second time in the nation's history. At the same time Congress passed a resolution of Daniel Webster, an ardent proponent of hard money, that after February 20, 1817 tax payments would only be accepted in specie, Bank of Second America banknotes, Treasury notes, or state paper currency that was convertible into gold or silver. In essence, the currency of the Second Bank of America was legal tender because it could be used to pay taxes to the government.

The Second Bank of the United States opened its doors in Philadelphia on January 7, 1817 with a twenty year charter. It would eventually have 29 branch offices in major cities across the United States which gave it a truly national reach. Like the First Bank of the United States, the Second Bank of the United States was a private bank with public functions. As a commercial bank it would accept deposits and extend loans to individuals and businesses, and on behalf of the government, it would accept the government's tax deposits, disburse the government's payments, make loans to the government, and help the government issue debt to the public. Twenty percent of the bank's capitalization of $35 million was held by the government, and eighty percent was owned by private investors. Five of the twenty five members of the bank's Board of Directors would be appointed by the President of the U.S. and confirmed by the Senate. The bank's loan rate could not exceed **6%.** In return for the government's promise not to establish another national bank, the government would receive a payment of 1.5 million.

After operating for only a year and a half, the bank was on the brink of collapse because the bank's policies contributed to the recession of

1819 - the first major economic crisis of the United States. The Second Bank of the United States had made too many loans at a time when there was a net outflow of specie because of a trade deficit; the balance of trade was not in favor of the U.S. William Jones was ousted and replaced by Langdon Cheves who was appointed President of the bank in 1819. Congress ordered an investigation into the bank's operations to uncover the bank's problems. The bank was forced to call in loans and curtail its lending, and the consequent contraction of credit that followed was responsible for bank failures, bankruptcies, foreclosures, a sharp decline in manufacturing, and a slump in agriculture. The bank survived the panic of 1819, but in the words of economic historian William M. Gouge, in his book A Short History of Paper Money and Banking in the United States, (page 110) "the bank was saved, and the people were ruined."

Pennsylvania banker Nicholas Biddle took over the reins of the Bank in 1822 and under his leadership the Second Bank of the United States helped to stabilize the economy until the panic of 1825 was activated by a stock market crash due to highly speculative investments in South America. This crisis severely affected England, but caused an economic slump in the United States also. Apart for a brief recession during 1933-34, the economy continued to expand as the charter of the Second Bank of the United States came close to its end in 1836.

Andrew Jackson defeated incumbent President John Quincy Adams in 1828, and after assuming office, President Jackson made his opposition to the bank clear right from the start. Although Nicholas Biddle supported President Andrew Jackson's election in 1928, and many people considered the bank as indispensable for the country, President Jackson nonetheless remained an implacable foe of the bank, an enemy determined to kill the bank. Four years before the charter of the bank was due to expire, Congressmen in favor of the bank's re-charter prepared a bank renewal bill for a 15 year extension of the bank's charter. Although it did not command a two thirds majority to override a presidential veto, the bill passed both the House and the Senate, and was presented to the President on July 4, 1832. Stating his objections to the bill, President Jackson returned the bill to the Senate unsigned on July 10, 1832. In his message, President Andrew Jackson wrote:

"A bank of the United States is in many respects convenient for the

Government and for the people. Entertaining this opinion, and deeply impressed with the belief that some of the powers and privileges possessed by the existing bank are unauthorized by the Constitution, subversive of the rights of the States, and dangerous to the liberties of the people, I felt it my duty... to call to the attention of Congress to the practicability of organizing an institution combining its advantages and obviating these objections. I sincerely regret that in the act before me I can perceive none of those modifications of the bank charter which are necessary, in my opinion, to make it compatible with justice, with sound policy, or with the Constitution of our country."

It seems from the above veto message that President Andrew Jackson was opposed to the Second Bank of the United States, but was not against a national central bank per se. If changes to the bank's powers, privileges, and independence had been made prior to presenting the bank bill to the President, and if these changes had satisfied the President, it is quite possible that President Andrew Jackson might not have vetoed such a modified bank bill. When Congress was in recess in the summer of 1933, Jackson ordered his Treasury Secretary to remove all government funds from the Second Bank of the United States and then place the funds in several state banks which were referred to as 'pet banks'. Congress censured President Andrew Jackson for refusing to provide a document related to the withdrawal of federal funds from the Second Bank of the United States. This was the first and only time that a U.S. President has ever been censured, although the censure was later expunged from the record by Democrats.

No other bank bill was presented in the next four years during President Jackson's second term in office, and so the charter of the Second Bank of the United States finally expired in 1836. In February 1836 the Second Bank of the United States became a state bank with a Pennsylvania charter. It was severely affected by the panic of 1837, and in 1841 the bank was permanently closed.

# FREE BANKING FROM 1836 TO 1863

From 1830 to 1836 speculators purchased, from the U.S. government, millions of acres of land that had been taken by force from Native Americans who owned the land. Land sales skyrocketed from 4.8 million in 1834 to 14.7 million in 1835 and then to 24.8 million in 1836 - a five fold increase during this period. So much land was sold and so much money flowed into the Treasury's coffers that the United States ended up with a surplus for the first time in the nation's history. President Andrew Jackson was able to reach an important milestone in his life: he had finally succeeded in paying off the nation's debt. At the same time Jackson was concerned about the sheer volume of state bank notes in circulation that was fueling the purchase of land. To reduce the flood of paper money that was funding this excessive speculation in land, Jackson promulgated the Specie Circular, which was an executive order that required payment for federal land in gold and silver only. No paper money would be accepted for purchase of land on or after August 15, 1836. The specie Circular was one of Jackson's the last acts before leaving office, hence the consequences of this act would be faced by the next President of the country.

Ten days before the end of President Andrew Jackson's term in office, a bill to annul the Specie Circular which had passed the House 143 to 59, and the Senate 41 to 5, was sent to the President for his signature. Without signing the bill, President Andrew Jackson sent it to the State Department at 11:45 PM on March 3, 1837. The next day, March 4, 1837 Martin Van Buren took over the presidency from Andrew Jackson.

Martin Van Buren, a descendant of Dutch immigrants, was the eighth

President of the United States, and the first President whose ancestors were not primarily of British origin. After he won the Presidential election of 1836 by getting 762,678 popular votes and 170 electoral votes, his incoming administration was immediately confronted with the serious after effects of the Specie Circular ordered by Jackson on July 11, 1836. After the Specie Circular became effective, land sales plummeted with a concomitant loss of revenues for state governments, particularly those in the west. 343 banks out of 850 banks failed completely, and another 62 banks failed partially. Innumerable businesses, factories, and mines closed permanently, unemployment skyrocketed, and people were rioting for food and bread. By causing a severe contraction of credit, the Specie Circular was highly deflationary, and it drastically reduced the amount of paper money in circulation. However, the Specie Circular was only partly to blame for the depression that lasted until 1844. The late historian William Graham Sumner wrote:

"At the session of 1835-36 Benton tried to get a resolution passed that nothing but gold or silver should be taken for public lands. He did not succeed. After Congress adjourned, July 11, 1836, the Secretary of the Treasury issued, by the President's order, a circular to all the land offices, known afterwards as the "Specie Circular," ordering that only gold, or silver, or land scrip should be received extraordinary rate. Lands were sold for $4,800,000 in 1834; for $14,700,000 in 1835; for $24,800,000 in 1836. The receipts for the lands consisted largely of notes of irresponsible banks. Land speculators organized a "bank," got it appointed a deposit bank, if they could, issued notes, borrowed them and bought land; the notes were deposited; they borrowed them again, and so on indefinitely. The guarantees required of the deposit banks were idle against such a scheme. There was, of course, little specie in the West on account of the flood of paper there. The circular caused inconvenience, and bad temper on the part of those who were checked in their transactions. It also caused trouble and expense in transporting specie from the East, and it no doubt made a demand for specie in the East against the banks there. In the existing state of the eastern banks this demand was probably just the touch needed to push down the rickety pretense of solvency which they were keeping up. Specie could not be drawn from Europe, except by a great fall in prices and a large contraction of the currency. Either through demand for specie or fall in prices, the inflated currency must collapse, and the crisis was at hand. Moreover, the banks were under notice to surrender, on January 1st, one fourth of the public deposits. Thousands of people who were carrying commodities or property for a rise, or who were engaged in enterprises, to finish which they depended on bank loans, found themselves arrested by the exorbitant rate for loans. The speculative period in England had also run its course, and the inflation here could no longer be sustained by borrowing there. From all these facts, it is plain that the specie circular may have played the role of the spark which produces an explosion, when all the conditions and the materials have been prepared; but those who called the circular the cause of the crisis made a mistake which is only too common in the criticism of economic events."

During the panic of 1837 many banks holding government funds collapsed, as a result of which President Van Buren wanted to set up an independent treasury which would, in effect, separate the U.S. Treasury from banking. William M. Gouge, a political economist specializing in monetary and banking theory, was the real author of the idea of an independent treasury which could enable the government to hold its money in the form of gold and silver in its treasury building and in sub treasuries in different cities. The bill for an Independent Treasury did not muster enough votes for passage in 1837, 1838, and 1839. On June 30, 1840 Congress voted 124 to 107 in favor of the Independent Treasury bill, and President Van Buren signed the Independent Treasury bill into law on July 4, 1840. The Democratic party called this the "second declaration of independence".

William Henry Harrison, an American military officer, was sworn into office on March 4, 1841 as the ninth President of the United States. He was the last President born as a British subject and his term in office lasted only 31 days as he died from complications of pneumonia in Washington DC on April 4, 1841. After President Harrison's death, vice President John Tyler became the tenth President and the first to assume the presidency without actually being elected. The Independent Treasury law was promptly repealed by Congress in 1841 after John Tyler became the President of the United States.

The Democrats emerged from the elections of 1844 with a Congressional majority and with James K. Polk as the eleventh President of the United

States. For President Polk, an independent treasury was the cornerstone of his economic agenda, and he vigorously pushed a bill through Congress for its reestablishment, which he signed into law on August 6, 1846.

The main strength of the Independent Treasury system lay in the fact that the safety of federal funds could now be assured because these funds would no longer be in private banks, and could no longer be used by a private bank for speculative purposes. The main weakness of the Independent Treasury system was that accumulation of specie in treasury and sub treasury vaults would reduce the amount of specie available in the nation's economy thereby contracting credit and reducing production and trade. During periods of economic distress, banks would suspend specie payments, yet the government had to be paid in specie. It was increasingly difficult to find the specie with which to pay the government during a recessionary period. While it was easy in theory to separate the Treasury from the banking system, it was far more difficult in practice to accomplish such a separation without undesirable consequences. It was impossible to divorce the operations of the treasury department from the financial system because specie payments to and from the government directly affected the quantity of specie in the economy and thus the availability of credit in the money market.

Before the free banking era began in 1837, a bank charter from the state was required in order to open a bank. Federal charters for banks were only available after the National Currency Act was enacted in 1863. A bank charter from a state had to be authorized by that state's legislature, which in real life meant that anyone who wanted to start a bank needed to have proper political connections. There was a great demand for these bank charters because there were no minimum reserve requirements in those days, and a state bank could print an unlimited number of bank notes. A bank charter was really a license to print paper currency without any limit.

In 1937 the state of Michigan started the free banking era by becoming the first state to grant a bank charter without an act of the state legislature. Thus the availability of bank charters was not restricted to only those with political connections. In fact the process of obtaining a bank charter became much simpler, and there were no cumbersome requirements for getting the charter. The example of Michigan was followed by the state of New York which passed a free banking law in 1838. Eighteen other states had free banking laws by 1860. The New York law contained the stipulation that bank notes issued by a bank had to be backed by government bonds, a requirement that was designed to protect the legitimate interests of depositors and banknote holders. New York also organized a state managed fund, something similar to deposit insurance, in which member banks made a contribution, so that depositors and holders of banknotes could be reimbursed in the event of a bank's failure. Louisiana passed a free banking law in 1842 which required banks to hold a third of their assets in cash, something similar to a reserve requirement.

Free banking laws were enacted in other states during this period, but there not much regulation in these laws. Consequently banks proliferated in those states, and unchecked by regulation or oversight, banks issued banknotes far in excess of their stock of specie. Some banks known as wildcat banks purposely located themselves in remote areas to make redemption of their bank notes difficult. Wildcat banks were started by unscrupulous bankers for the sole purpose of defrauding the public by printing currency that they could never redeem in specie. After raking in their illegitimate profits, these bankers would close their banks and flee with the assets. Approximately half of all free banks in New York, Indiana, Wisconsin, and Minnesota failed between 1838 and 1863. Numerous free banks in other states also failed between 1836 and 1863.

# THE CIVIL WAR AND THE NATIONAL BANKING SYSTEM

Because of its inherent weaknesses, the Independent Treasury system could not cope with the exigencies of the American Civil War that broke out on April 12, 1861 when the first shots of the conflict were fired in anger at the U.S. fortress of Fort Sumter in Charleston, South Carolina. Earlier in November of 1860, Abraham Lincoln, the leader of the new Republican party, had defeated rival Democrat Stephen A. Douglas to become the 16th President of the United States. Even before Lincoln had been sworn in as President in March of 1861, the seven Southern states of Alabama, Florida, Georgia, Louisiana, Mississippi, South Carolina, and Texas, had declared their secession from the United States in February of 1861 to form the Confederate States of America. After the Civil War began, Arkansas, North Carolina, Tennessee, and Virginia also joined the Confederacy in April of 1861. The western part of Virginia remained loyal to the Union, and was admitted to the Union as the state of West Virginia on June 20, 1863 during the civil war. Abraham Lincoln was an outspoken critic and a fierce opponent of the institution of slavery upon which the prosperity of the South depended. To these Southern states, the election of Abraham Lincoln posed a mortal threat to their way of life, which was based, more than anything else, on slavery.

Within a few months after the war started, it was obvious that the union government's meager income from taxes and excises could not possibly pay for the costs of prosecuting the war. President Lincoln explored the possibility of obtaining loans from major banks in New York City which asked for interest rates of 24 to 36 percent. Rather than pay such exorbitant interest, President Lincoln decided to look for other solutions. In July of 1861 Congress authorized the issuance of $50 million in Demand notes which were printed on both sides, with one side printed in green ink - hence the name 'greenbacks'. These notes did not pay interest, but could be used to pay customs duties, and were redeemable in gold or silver. Initially these notes were not legal tender, but in March of 1862 Demand notes became legal tender. Demand notes were inadequate for financing the war effort, and so on February 25, 1862 Congress passed the first Legal Tender Act for the issuance of $150 million in United States notes which were full Legal Tender but not redeemable in specie. The United States notes were also printed on both sides, with green ink on one side, and were also referred to as 'greenbacks'. Second and third issues of $150 million each were authorized in July of 1862, and in early 1863, respectively, so that the amount of 'greenbacks' in circulation amounted to about $450 million in 1864. The printing of greenbacks financed $432 million out of the total accumulated deficit of $2.614 billion during the Civil War. The remainder was financed by issuing public debt.

Treasury Secretary Salmon Chase granted a monopoly to Jay Cooke and Co to underwrite the public debt, and in mid 1863 the Union government stopped printing greenbacks and started to issue inordinate amounts of public debt using the services of Jay Cooke & Co. The late Edward Kirkland, describing Cooke's efforts, wrote in his book, Industry Comes of Age: Business, Labor & Public Policy (pages 20-21):

"With characteristic optimism, he flung himself into a bond crusade. He recruited a small army of 2,500 sub-agents among bankers, insurance men, and community leaders and kept them inspired and informed by mail and telegraph. He taught the American people to buy bonds, using lavish advertising in newspapers, broadsides, and posters. God, destiny, duty, courage, patriotism - all summoned "Farmers, Mechanics, and Capitalists" to invest in loans."

Without creating another central bank, the Union government wanted to be able to exert some control over the banking industry, and so in 1863 it decided to create a system of national banks which it could regulate and control. By means of this system of national banks, the federal government expected to establish a uniform national currency, and in the process create a market for its bonds with which to defray the costs of the war.

The sale of government debt was facilitated by the National Currency Act of 1863 which created national banks and required these national banks to hold at least a third of their capital in government bonds. National banks could issue banknotes, but every $90 worth of these banknotes had to be backed by $100 worth of Union government bonds. This requirement meant that in the new national banking system which replaced the pre-Civil war state banking system, national banks could only print banknotes if they owned government bonds. A national bank had to deposit sufficient government securities as collateral with the U.S. Treasury prior to issuance of any banknotes, and the total amount of paper currency issued by this national bank could not exceed 90% of the value of government bonds that this national bank had on deposit.

The National Banking Act of 1864 established the Office of the Comptroller of the Currency whose job was to determine the soundness of national banks through periodic bank examinations. The Comptroller of the Currency could grant a charter for a national bank to anyone qualified to receive the charter, that is to anyone who could meet the stiff legal requirements of being eligible for a federal charter. The minimum capital requirements ranged from $50,000 for rural banks to $200,000 for banks in larger cities. The national banking system created three classes of national banks: central reserve city banks in New York, reserve city banks in other cities with a population of more than half million, and the rest were classified as country banks.

Although the Union government preferred to have national banks rather than state banks, the latter disliked becoming national banks because national banks needed much more start up capital, and had higher reserve requirements than state banks. National banks were under the jurisdiction of the federal government and faced a myriad number of federal rules, regulations, and restrictions, whereas a state bank was not regulated or controlled by the federal government. In order to induce state banks to become national banks, the Union government passed the National Banking Act of 1865 which imposed an annual 10% federal excise tax on state banknotes. As a result of this legislation most state banknotes disappeared because it became unprofitable for state banks to issue banknotes. State banks countered by replacing banknotes with checks on which the 10% tax did not apply. Instead of banknotes, state banks used checking accounts to create more money than what they had in reserves of gold and silver.

President Abraham Lincoln was still alive and was able to know the outcome of the war when General Robert E. Lee surrendered to General Ulysses S. Grant at Appomattox in Virginia on April 9, 1865. But on April 14, 1865 Lincoln was shot in the back of the head by John Wilkes Booth at Ford's Theater in Washington DC, and died the next morning on April 15, 1865. He became the first U.S. President to be assassinated, and was succeeded by Vice President Andrew Johnson as the 17th President of the United States.

The banking industry continued to expand after the Civil War with the number of national banks increasing from 1,294 in 1865 to 1,968 in 1873, and the number of state banks increasing from 349 in 1865 to 1,330 in 1873. The primary cause of the panic of 1873 was excessive investment in the nation's railways. The railway industry was the country's largest employer apart from agriculture, and growth in this industry was propelled by vast government land grants and subsidies. The Northern Pacific Railroad was the recipient of the largest federal subsidy - it received a land grant of 47 million acres. Investors realized very high rates of return during the early phase of the development of railroads, but in later years, although investment in the railroad industry continued unabated, new railroad projects began to yield diminishing rates of return on investment.

In the summer of 1873, the stock market crashed in Vienna, the capital of the Austro-Hungarian Empire, and this event compelled large European investors to reduce their portfolio of American securities, especially railroad bonds. This in turn lowered the price of railroad bonds and financing became difficult for railroad companies. Without being able to refinance debt that had matured, many of these companies had to default on their debt, and without being able to borrow money to continue business operations, many of these railroad companies had to close. This was the situation faced by Jay Cooke & Co which had invested extensively in the Northern Pacific Railroad. Jay Cooke & Co declared bankruptcy on September 18, 1873 and the Northern Pacific Railroad then collapsed. Two days later, on September 20, 1873 the New York Stock Exchange closed for the first time in its history, and trading on the exchange was suspended for ten days. Investors lost confidence in banks throughout the country, resulting in the failure of more than 100 banks. The panic of 1873 marked the start of a depression that would last for the next five years during which time tens of thousands of businesses would close, and hundreds of thousands of workers would lose their jobs.

By printing greenbacks not backed by specie, the U.S. went off the gold standard in July of 1861 and remained off the gold standard until 1879. After President Ulysses S. Grant was reelected for a second term in 1872, his administration passed the Specie Resumption Act in 1875, a law which would return the United States dollar to the gold standard on the first day of 1879. After returning to the gold standard, the decade of 1879 to 1889 was a decade of solid economic growth for the United States. From 1879 to 1889, during a period of falling prices, nominal wages nonetheless increased 23%, which translated into a significant increase in real wages for the U.S. worker, and an elevated level of purchasing power for the public at large. During this prosperous period, two more panics occurred that were both limited in impact and in scope - the panic of 1884 and the panic of 1890.

The Marine National Bank, the brokerage firm of Grant and Wade, and the Metropolitan National Bank, all failed in 1894 and caused the panic of 1884, but timely intervention by the New York Clearing House limited the impact of this panic. The panic of 1890 had its origin in the failure of the brokerage firm of Decker, Howell, and Co. in November of 1890, which precipitated a run on its bank, the Bank of North America. The crisis was contained by the intervention of J. P. Morgan who was able to organize a coalition of nine New York City banks to succor the Bank of North America.

When Grover Cleveland was inaugurated to the presidency in March of 1893, business activity in the nation's economy was slackening. Overbuilding in the construction industry had slowed investment in construction, and agricultural overproduction had resulted in the fall in prices of agricultural commodities, to the detriment of farmers. Low prices for their agricultural products created an untenable situation for farmers who not only suffered from a loss of purchasing power, but who also lost the wherewithal to service their farm mortgages. At this time, the failure of two of the nation's biggest employers, the Philadelphia and Reading Railroad and the National Cordage Company ignited the panic of 1893 which proved to be a national economic disaster. It triggered a stock and bond market slump, and bankrupted innumerable businesses as a result of banks and investment firms calling in their loans. Eventually more than fifteen thousand business firms including banks, railroads, and steel mills were wiped out. The unemployment rate climbed to twenty five percent, unemployed workers became homeless, and many people had no money to buy food. A protest march was organized from Ohio to Washington but the local police broke up the march and arrested its leaders. It would take four years for the panic to end in 1897.

# THE PANIC OF 1907

In 1907 Fritz Augustus Heinze opened the United Copper Company at 42 Broadway in the city of New York, and entered into a partnership with Charles Wyman Morse who controlled the Bank of North America, the Mercantile National Bank, and the Knickerbocker Trust Co. The United Copper Company was set up purely for speculation; the company did not produce any copper. Otto Heinze and Arthur Heinze, two brothers of Fritz A. Heinze, owned a brokerage firm also located at 42 Broadway. Otto's strategy for cornering the stock of United Copper required the Heinze family to aggressively buy stock and call options in United Copper to cause its stock price to rise, and thus induce other speculators into going short. In order to 'short' a stock, an investor borrows and sells stock at a high price betting that the stock price will fall, and if the stock price does fall, the investor makes a profit by buying and replacing the borrowed stock at the lower price. If they could corner the market for United Copper stock, they could then exercise their call option and compel the short sellers to replace the borrowed stock at the higher share price.

The plan to corner the market required much more money than the combined financial resources of the Heinze family and Charles Morse, and so the two bothers Otto and Augustus Heinze, and Charles Morse approached Charles T. Barney, the president of the Knickerbocker Trust Company, for assistance. Barney refused to help, but Otto was not deterred, and proceeded to put his plan into action. He started purchasing shares of United Copper so aggressively on Monday, October 14 that its stock price climbed from $39 to $52 in a single day. When the stock price reached $60 the next day, Tuesday, October 15, he exercised his call options for short sellers to return the borrowed stock. Short sellers, though, were able to find shares of United Copper stock in the market that did not belong to the Heinze family, and therefore had no difficulty in returning the borrowed stock. The attempt to corner the market for United Copper stock had failed. It was the result of a gross miscalculation by the Heinze brothers and Charles W. Morse who had completely misread the market. As John S. Gordon writes in his book, The Great Game: The Emergence of Wall Street as a World Power: 1653-2000 (page 190):

"On Monday October 14, the shorts began to cover, and while all other copper stocks declined, United shot up from 37½ to 60. Heinze was sure that triumph was at hand and sent word to his various brokers to exercise his call options. But the brokers were unaccountably slow to act. Time was of the essence but they dawdled about sending out the notices. Further, stories began appearing in the papers about UC, questioning its finances. There is no proof that Standard Oil was involved in either the delays or the bad press, but few on Wall Street at the time, and few historians since, have doubted that they were both orchestrated from 26 Broadway, the headquarters of the Rockefeller empire."

By the end of the day's trading on Tuesday, October 15, United Copper stock closed at $30, and the next day, Wednesday October 16, it plummeted to $10. The Heinze brothers lost millions and were financially finished. The State Savings Bank of Butte, owned by Fritz A. Heinze became insolvent as a consequence of United Copper's collapse, and the Board of the Mercantile National Bank immediately ousted him from the presidency of the bank. Frantic depositors began a run on the Mercantile National Bank and on two banks owned by Charles W. Morse: the Bank of North America, and the New Amsterdam National Bank. After depositors started withdrawing their funds from the Knickerbocker Trust Company on Friday October 18, the Board of Knickerbocker forced Charles T. Barney to resign on Monday October 21. On the same day, the National Bank of Commerce announced that it would stop clearing checks for the Knickerbocker Trust Company. This announcement exacerbated the situation for Knickerbocker because it precipitated a run by worried depositors the following day. Exhausted after paying out $8 million to depositors in the morning of October 22, the

Knickerbocker Trust Company suspended operations at noon on Tuesday October 22.

The suspension of the Knickerbocker Trust Company lit the fuse that sparked the financial calamity of 1907 in New York City. The financial catastrophe completely ruined numerous small banks, but even large trusts such as the Trust Company of America and the Lincoln Trust Company were severely affected. A litany of failed banks dotted the landscape: First National Bank of Brooklyn, International Trust Company of New York, Union Trust Company of Providence, Empire City Savings Bank, Borough Bank of Brooklyn, Jenkins Trust Company of Brooklyn, Twelfth Ward Bank, and Hamilton Bank of New York. Banks and trusts slashed their lending, causing a credit crunch so severe that the interest rate for loans to brokers at the stock exchange sky rocketed to as high as 70%, as stock prices declined to record lows.

For a period of two weeks from October 22 to November 4, 1907, the Trust Company of America experienced a run during which it paid out $47.5 million out of $60 million in deposits. Fearing that the collapse of the Trust Company of America and the Lincoln Trust Company was a threat to the survival of the financial system of New York, a group of five prominent trust company presidents appealed to J.P. Morgan for help. Benjamin Strong, a financial expert from the Bankers Trust Company was sent to determine the financial condition of the Trust Company of America. After he reported to Morgan that the bank in question was basically sound, Morgan provided immediate assistance of around $3 million dollars which enabled the Trust Company of America to continue operating.

John D. Rockefeller joined the effort to help the trusts by providing $10 million, and Secretary Treasury George Cortelyou deposited a total of $37.6 million of the U.S. government's money in New York national banks to help contain the crisis. At this point the U.S. government had only $5 million left in its coffers, and could not help with any more money for the remainder of the crisis. Through Morgan's efforts, both the Trust Company of America and the Lincoln Trust Company received about $25 million in loans to survive during the crisis. J.P. Morgan organized a coalition of trust companies to aid the trust companies that were in trouble, and this helped to ameliorate the panic of 1907.

Before 1853, banks used to employ porters to go from bank to bank for the purpose of exchanging checks for bags of gold or silver coin. In response to the idea of a clearing house first published in an article by George D. Lyman, the New York Clearing House was established in October of 1853. Fifty two banks took part in the first exchange of checks worth about $22.6 million at the newly organized New York Clearing House at 14 Wall Street on October 11 of 1853. Soon afterwards, gold certificates replaced actual gold as a means of settlement, and so it was not necessary any more for porters to transport bags of gold from one bank to another.

The monetary system during the national banking era did not have a built in mechanism with which to expand the supply of currency rapidly if needed during a financial emergency. To circumvent this inherent deficiency in the monetary system that existed in 1907, a committee of the New York Clearinghouse met on October 26 of 1907 to consider the issuance of loan certificates in order to increase liquidity. These loan certificates were authorized and issued for the first time on October 26, 1907. As a result of this innovation, banks could use loan certificates instead of their reserves of currency to settle their accounts with each other, thus freeing up the currency needed to satisfy depositors' demands for cash. Loan certificates were not legal tender and could not legally be used as cash by the public; they could only be used by banks to clear checks and to settle accounts with each other. For the entire duration of the financial crisis of 1907, approximately $500 million of these loan certificates circulated among banks as a means of settling balances, and as a method of payment.

The loan certificates of 1907 were a forerunner of what is today known as discount window loans at a Federal Reserve Bank. The discount window permits eligible financial institutions to borrow funds on a short term basis from the Federal Reserve. The expression 'discount window' has its origin in the fact that it was customary for a bank official to appear at the teller window of a Federal Reserve Bank to borrow money for his bank.

There are some remarkable similarities between the panic of 1907 and the Great Recession of 2008. In 1907 there were runs by depositors on financial institutions such as large trust companies that were not members of the New York Clearing House, and similarly in 2008 the financial turmoil involved financial institutions that were not members of the

Federal Reserve. In both crises, the trouble started with institutions that were not members of payments clearing systems, but eventually spread to other institutions in the financial system, regardless of whether or not they were members of the New York Clearing House in 1907 or of the Federal Reserve in 2008.

During the panic of 1907, trust companies without access to the New York Clearing House provided short term loans to brokers to enable them to purchase stock in the stock market, and a similar role was played by shadow banks during the Great Recession. Shadow banks normally do not have banking licenses, do not accept deposits from depositors, are not supported by central bank funding, are not covered by deposit insurance, and are not regulated like traditional banks. Yet they function like traditional banks in the sense that they provide credit and liquidity. Shadow banks such as hedge funds, money market funds, private equity funds, structured investment vehicles, exchange traded funds, etc. provided short term loans to investment banks and also acted as intermediaries between lenders and borrowers by channeling short term loans from lenders such as pension funds to borrowers such as investment banks during the Great Recession.

The panic of 1907 was a financial and economic catastrophe so severe that industrial output declined by 17%, GNP decreased by 12%, and the rate of employment climbed to 20%. Millions of people lost their deposits as thousands of banks failed. There were calls for a sweeping reform of the monetary system. Intellectuals, politicians, and bankers were all in favor of a new banking system similar to the European system of central banking. J.P. Morgan, a man of phenomenal wealth, had helped to alleviate the crisis by extending loans from his own pocket to important banks in distress. What if there was no one like John P. Morgan available to mitigate the next financial crisis? A consensus began to form that a financial institution that could inject emergency liquidity into the system, and act as a lender of last resort was absolutely necessary to obviate future panics.

# THE NATIONAL MONETARY COMMISSION

Senator Nelson W. Aldrich, a Republican Senator from Rhode Island, and Representative Edward Vreeland, a Republican Congressman from New York, sponsored the bill that was signed into law as the Aldrich-Vreeland Act on May 30, 1908. This law, enacted in the wake of the crisis of 1907, allowed groups of ten or more national banks to issue emergency currency which could be backed by government bonds or other securities that the banks had in their possession. The Aldrich-Vreeland Act also created the National Monetary Commission, a bipartisan group of eighteen Congressmen, consisting of nine members of the Senate and nine members of the House of Representatives, to study the banking history and laws of the United States, Canada, Mexico, and a number of financially important European countries, in an effort to understand the defects and deficiencies inherent in the monetary system of the United States at that time. The National Monetary Commission was entrusted with the task of delving into the banking arrangements, methods, and practices of England, France, and Germany by means of on site visits to the financial institutions, first hand observation, talks with important bank officials, and interviews of key personnel. On the basis of its study, research, inquiry, and investigation, the National Monetary Commission was expected to prepare and submit reports to Congress on the overhaul of the current monetary system of the United States. Such reports needed to outline the changes that were necessary, and specify the steps that had to be taken in order to reform the existing monetary system of the United States.

Aldrich hired Dr. Abraham Piatt Andrew, Assistant Professor of Economics at Harvard, who took a two year leave of absence from Harvard University to join Aldrich's team at a salary of $3,000. In addition to his strong academic credentials, Dr. Andrew had written a paper in 1907 that correctly predicted the financial crisis that began in October of 1907. Aldrich also recruited Henry P. Davison, a senior partner at J.P. Morgan & Company, as an advisor. Eight members of this group, which included Aldrich, Andrew, and Davison, would journey across the Atlantic to Europe on a fact finding mission to unlock the secrets of European central banking. Shortly after Aldrich and his party had arrived at the port of Plymouth, England on August 10, 1908, Nelson Aldrich requested George Reynolds, head of the Continental National Bank of Chicago, to join his team. George Reynolds was on vacation in Italy when Aldrich called him, but Reynolds promptly cut short his vacation in Italy to join Aldrich.

The world's first central bank, the Sveriges Riksbank was founded in 1668 in Stockholm to provide loans to the King of Sweden. It was followed by the establishment of the Bank of England in 1694 by Scottish banker William Paterson, also for the purpose of loaning money to the English monarchy which badly lacked the funds to pursue its war with France. In 1946 the British Government nationalized the Bank of England, and in 1998 it became an independent public organization which is now wholly owned by the Government Legal Department of the United Kingdom with the power to independently set monetary policy. The Bank of France or the Banque de France as it is known in France, was founded by private bankers in 1800 with the support of Napoleon Bonaparte. The Banque de France was the sole issuer of banknotes in France until 1815, when Napoleon was defeated by the Duke of Wellington at Waterloo in Belgium on June 18, 1815. The Reichsbank was founded on January 1, 1876 as a privately owned bank controlled by the Reich government, and served as the central bank of Germany until 1945, when Germany lost the second world war. Aldrich and his team started their mission with interviews of important bank officials at the Bank of England in London. After London they traveled to Berlin and then to Paris by train to meet and interview important people in the central banks of these two countries where they engaged in talks and conducted interviews with the help of interpreters. In his book, America's Bank: The Epic Struggle To Create The Federal Reserve (pages 84-85) author Roger Lowenstein writes:

"Aldrich focused on the big three of European banking - England, Germany, and France. Each of these central banks was owned by private shareholders and held the national reserve, but in important ways they differed. The Bank of France possessed far more gold - more in fact, than the other two combined. Also the French banks were controlled by the state; England's was defiantly independent. Surprisingly, directors of the latter were wealthy merchants rather than bankers. In Germany, management was in the hands of trained professionals - experts such as Warburg. The German chancellor held supreme power over the Reichsbank but rarely used it."

Aldrich and his team were taken aback by what they heard at the central banks of these three countries. Officials at the central banks of London, Paris, and Berlin described the operations of their banks as vital to the national interests of their respective countries. They explained that the policies of their banks were designed primarily to serve the national interest, with the interests of private shareholders of the central bank as being subservient to the national interest. Aldrich and his team were unable to elicit straight forward answers to their questions from the European bankers. On the question of fractional reserve requirements, the Europeans' vague response was that confidence in their central banking system was such that there was no need for strict rules and regulations regarding required reserves. When Aldrich asked to know the precise mechanism by means of which the Bank of England manipulated the money supply, a bank official explained that this happened "automatically" when bills of trade were exchanged for Bank of England paper currency. At the Reichsbank, a German banker explained that it was imperative for the central bank to exchange German currency for bank loans without being fettered by strict rules because otherwise a serious financial crisis might be the result. Aldrich again posited the same question about fractional reserve requirements at the French central bank. The governor of the Banque de France, Monsieur Pallain, responded that there were no reserve requirements in his country because the Banque de France would have no hesitation in quickly exchanging cash for assets if it ever became necessary.

In June of 1908, Secretary of War William Howard Taft, who publicly supported the National Monetary Commission led by Aldrich, was nominated by the Republicans to run for the presidency. The Democrats nominated William Jennings Bryan, whose ideas regarding monetary reform were quite different from that of Aldrich and his monetary commission. Before he left for Europe, Aldrich felt that the work of the National Monetary Commission would be futile if Bryan managed to win the presidential election. After an absence of eleven weeks, Senator Aldrich returned to New York from his trip to Europe on October 20, 1908, and his anxiety was greatly relieved when William Howard Taft defeated Bryan on November 3, 1908, to become the 27th President of the United States in March of 1909.

Aldrich was greatly impressed by what he thought was the superior central banking system of Europe. He returned from his study tour of Europe with the conviction that the United States was in dire need of a central bank, although he was not sure if it would be politically possible to establish a central bank in the United States, given the fierce opposition in the minds of the public to the concept of an all powerful entity in the form of a central bank. Aldrich decided to retire when his term of office expired in 1911, and made up his mind to devote the remainder of his term in office on monetary reform.

The Republicans had won the last four presidential elections since 1896 when William Mckinley defeated William Jennings Bryan. In the mid term elections of 1910, in the middle of President William Howard Taft's presidency, the Democrats won control of the House of Representatives by winning 230 out of 394 seats. The Democrats gained 57 seats in the House which gave them outright control of the House, and they gained 10 seats in the Senate, which allowed them to control the Senate in conjunction with progressive Republicans. The Democrats also won the governorships of New York and New Jersey for the first time since 1892, with Woodrow Wilson becoming the new governor of New Jersey. Aldrich was now confronted with a new political reality. The monetary reform plan that he intended to draft shortly, would now have to be presented to a Congress dominated not by Republicans, but by Democrats, from whom he did not expect a fair and impartial evaluation of the monetary reform plan that he was about to prepare.

Nelson Aldrich intended to draft his monetary reform plan with the aid of private bankers, but he also realized that his monetary reform plan would be doomed the moment it became known that he had enlisted the help of Wall Street bankers. Therefore, he organized a group that would meet in total secrecy in November of 1910, at the private resort of John Pierpont Morgan in Jekyll Island, off the coast of Georgia. Besides Senator Aldrich there were five other people in the group: Frank Vanderlip, the President of the National City Bank of New York, Paul Warburg, a partner in Kuhn Loeb & Company, Henry P. Davison, a senior partner of the J.P. Morgan Company, Dr. Abraham Piatt Andrew who was now the Assistant Secretary of the U.S. Treasury, and Arthur Shelton, the personal secretary of Senator Aldrich. Accommodation had been arranged by Henry P. Davison for Aldrich and his party to stay at the exclusive Jekyll Island Club, founded in 1885 as one of the most exclusive and inaccessible clubs on earth. It was also arranged that no other guests should be present at this club during the time that Aldrich and his party occupied the main house of this club, a large and comfortable mansion of Victorian architecture. A hundred years later, Dr. Ben S. Bernanke, the Chairman of the Federal Reserve, went to Jekyll Island in November of 2010 to mark the 100th year of the original meeting. The Jekyll Island Club closed in 1942, but its former clubhouse and cottages remain as National Historic Landmarks.

At about 10 PM on this cold November night of 1910, members of this group arrived, one by one, at a railroad station in New Jersey, to board Senator Aldrich's private railcar attached to the end of a southbound train, to make the eight hundred mile rail journey which would take them to Brunswick via Atlanta and Savannah. At the small fishing village of Brunswick on the Atlantic seaboard, the party disembarked from the private railcar to board a launch that would ferry them across the sea to Jekyll Island. Because of its clandestine nature, and because it took 20 years for it to be publicly revealed in Aldrich's autobiography in 1930, the Jekyll Island meeting has been the basis of many conspiracy theories regarding the formation of the Federal Reserve System.

In 1952, Eustace Mullins was the first to reveal the secret meeting of a U.S. Senator, his private secretary, an Assistant Secretary of the U.S. Treasury, and three Wall Street bankers in an exclusive private resort on a secluded island in his book, Mullins on the Federal Reserve. In a later version of this book entitled., The Secrets of the Federal Reserve, published in 1991, Eustace Mullins writes on page 1:

"The delegation had left in a sealed railway car, with blinds drawn, for an undisclosed destination. They were led by Senator Nelson Aldrich, head of the National Monetary Commission. President Theodore Roosevelt had signed into law the bill creating the National Monetary Commission in 1908, after the tragic Panic of 1907 had resulted in a public outcry that the nation's monetary system be stabilized. Aldrich had led the members of the Commission on a two-year tour of Europe, spending some three hundred thousand dollars of public money. He had not yet made a report on the results of this trip, nor had he made any plan for banking reform".

G. Edward Griffin provides this summary in his 1994 book, The Creature for Jekyll Island: A Second Look at the Federal Reserve, on page 23:

'The basic plan for the Federal Reserve System was drafted at a secret meeting in November of 1910 at the private resort of J.P. Morgan on Jekyll Island off the coast of Georgia. Those who attended represented the great financial institutions of Wall Street and, indirectly, Europe as well. The reason for secrecy was simple. Had it been known that rival factions of the banking community had joined together, the public would have been alerted to the possibility that the bankers were plotting an agreement in restraint of trade - which, of course, is exactly what they were doing. What emerged was a cartel agreement with five objectives: stop the growing competition from the nation's newer banks; obtain a franchise to create money out of nothing for the purpose of lending; get control of the reserves of all banks so that the more reckless ones would not be exposed to currency drains and bank runs; get the taxpayer to pick up the cartel's inevitable losses; and convince Congress that the purpose was to protect the public. It was realized that the bankers would have to become partners with the politicians and that the structure of the cartel would have to be a central bank. The record shows that the Fed has failed to achieve its stated objectives. That is because those were never its true goals. As a banking cartel, and in terms of the five objectives stated above, it has been an unqualified success."

The Aldrich plan was released on January 17, 1911 and presented as the personal work of Senator Aldrich. The plan called for a fifty year charter of a Reserve Association of fifteen regional banks, located in major regions of the country, that was authorized by the federal government, but controlled by a board of private bankers. The Reserve Association would perform the role of a lender of last resort by supplying emergency loans to member banks in need of funds. It would provide an elastic currency by centralizing reserves, which means that instead of each bank holding its own reserve in its vault, the Reserve Association would hold the reserves of all member banks. It would issue a new national currency, with a government granted monopoly of the note issue, which would be equally interchangeable with demand deposits. In other words, a single bank, the Reserve Association, would have a monopoly on the note issue.

The real author of the Aldrich plan was, of course, not Senator Aldrich, but Paul Moritz Warburg, who was born on August 10, 1868 in Germany to a Jewish family that owned the banking firm of M.M. Warburg & Co in Hamburg. After working for Samuel Montague & Co in London, and for the Banque Russe pour le Commerce Etranger in Paris, Warburg started working for his family banking firm in Hamburg in 1891. In 1895 he married Nina Loeb, the daughter of an American financier of German-Jewish descent. In 1902 Paul and Nina Warburg moved to New York, where he joined his father in law's investment bank of Kuhn, Loeb, & Co. Professor Edwin Seligman, wrote in the Academy of Political Science, Proceedings, v. 4, No. 4, p. 387-90:

"It is known to very few how great is the indebtedness of the United States to Mr. Warburg. For it may be said without fear of contradiction that in its fundamental features the Federal Reserve Act is the work of Mr. Warburg more than any other man in the country. The existence of a Federal Reserve Board creates, in everything but in name, a real central bank. In the two fundamentals of command of reserves and of a discount policy, the Federal Reserve Act has frankly accepted the principle of the Aldrich bill, and these principles, as has been stated, were the creation of Mr. Warburg and Mr. Warburg alone."

# THE FEDERAL RESERVE ACT OF 1913

Nelson W. Aldrich, a Republican Senator from Rhode Island, and the Chairman of the Senate Finance Committee, was a wealthy man whose reputation had been tainted by charges of corruption. His daughter Abby Greene Aldrich was married to John D. Rockefeller, Jr in 1901. His grandson Nelson Aldrich Rockefeller was governor of New York from 1959 to 1973, and the vice president of the U.S. from 1974 to 1977 during the presidency of Gerald Ford.

Congress had set January 8, 1912 as the deadline for the submission of the National Monetary Commission report. Hours before this deadline in January of 1912, almost four years after the National Monetary Commission was created, the Head of the National Monetary Commission, Senator Nelson Aldrich, submitted his monetary reform plan in a legislative proposal to charter a "National Reserve Association of the United States". Congress was not in session on this day, and so Professor A.P. Andrew, on behalf of Senator Nelson Aldrich, went to the residence of the Vice President, and then to the residence of the Speaker of the House, to directly deliver to them, signed copies of the Aldrich Plan. After submitting its report, the National Monetary Commission became defunct, and passed into history.

The Aldrich Bill never came to a vote in Congress because the Democrats won control of the House in the mid term elections of 1910, and after the Aldrich bill was introduced in 1912, the Democrats wrested control of the Senate as well as the Presidency in the elections of 1912, with an election campaign based on opposition to the Aldrich plan. Woodrow Wilson who was elected as the 28th President of the United States in November of 1912, repudiated the Aldrich plan or the concept of any kind of a European-type central bank, although he was otherwise in favor of monetary reform and realized the importance of such reform for the United States. After his election victory, President Woodrow Wilson moderated his rhetoric, but reiterated that any monetary reform bill must originate within his administration and that such a bill must balance both private and public interests. He would not countenance a bill written by "a controlling group of bankers" whose primary objective would be to create a rigid centralized structure dominated and controlled by private bankers.

In February of 1912, in response to a growing concern over the increasing financial power of the so called 'money trusts', the Democratic Money Trust Caucus passed House Resolution 405 to launch a probe of the money trusts. The term 'money trust' was a reference to the collection of Wall Street bankers and financiers who exerted undue control and influence over the nation's finances. The investigation of the money trusts was entrusted to Congressman Arsene Paulin Pujo of Louisiana, who was himself a former member of the National Monetary Commission, and was at that time the Chairman of the Banking and Currency Committee. The Pujo investigation confirmed in early 1913 that there was indeed "a vast and growing control over money and credit" in the hands of a private Wall Street 'money trust'.

The Aldrich plan proposed the creation of a National Reserve Association consisting of 15 regional district branches, with 46 geographically dispersed directors, most of whom would be bankers. There would be local associations of banks, and these local associations of banks would be further grouped into regional associations. Any bank in the United States that could satisfy certain requirements could become a member of the National Reserve Association, but it was not compulsory for any bank to become a member of the NRA. The Aldrich plan did not refer to the NRA as a central bank, but in reality the great central banks of Europe, in particular the Reichsbank of Germany, that Aldrich and his colleagues had studied, shaped the design of the NRA. The National Reserve Association was a virtual prototype of the Reichsbank of Germany, and would perform the same functions as that of any major European central bank. It would hold and administer the bank reserves of the country, it would provide loans in exchange for commercial paper (commercial paper is a short term promissory note) to banks, it would print an elastic currency, and it would serve as a fiscal agent for the government.

As envisioned in the Aldrich plan, the control of the National Reserve Association would reside almost entirely in the hands of private bankers. The power and influence of the U.S. government over the National Reserve Association as proposed in the Aldrich Bill would be minuscule. According to author Peter Conti-Brown who writes in his book, The Power And Independence of the Federal Reserve, on page 17:

"In 1908, Congress passed the Aldrich-Vreeland Act, which created the National Monetary Commission with Aldrich at the head. The commission imagined a structure very different from the system the Federal Reserve Act eventually created. That structure, the National Reserve Association (NRA), was to be a mix of public and private appointments, but dramatically weighted toward the private. For example, the board of the NRA was to have forty six directors, forty two of whom - including its three executive officers - were to be appointed directly and indirectly by the banks. The government did not figure into the scene at all."

In the proposed 46-member Board of Directors of the National Reserve Association, only the Secretary of the Treasury, the Secretary of Agriculture, the Secretary of Commerce and Labor, and the Comptroller of the Currency would represent the U.S. government. Similarly, only the Governor and the Comptroller of the Board's nine member Executive Committee would represent the U.S. government. The absence of government oversight and control, and the lack of public ownership inherent in the Aldrich plan, made it quite obvious to Democrats that implementation of the National Reserve Association would greatly amplify and entrench the financial power of Wall Street bankers over the U.S. economy.

The National Monetary Commission attributed the series of financial panics that occurred in the United States prior to 1908, to i) an "inelastic currency", and to ii) the prevailing system of "pyramiding" of reserves which allowed a dollar of reserves to be created as reserves more than once.

As the Federal Reserve Bank of San Francisco explains on page 1 of its weekly letter of January 6, 1984, written by Verle B. Johnston:

"Under the National Banking System established in 1863, the nation's supply of currency consisted of a fixed amount of government currency (greenbacks) and notes issued by national banks. In principle, the amount of national banknotes in circulation could increase when the public's demand for currency rose, but it was felt that in practice the response was inadequate - that the supply of currency was too inelastic to respond to the demand for currency. In the eyes of many critics at the time, the problem of an inelastic currency was compounded by the practice of "pyramiding," in which country banks would place their reserves with city banks, who in turn would loan them out in the market. A shortage of currency in the country banks, sometimes just because of higher seasonal needs, would lead to calls for their funds from city banks, which if the extra demand was great enough, would find themselves with insufficient cash to meet these calls. In such situations, country banks might have to close their doors, precipitating depositor panics that spread to other banks."

In addition to the lack of government oversight and control embodied in the organizational structure of the Aldrich plan, the incoming administration of President Woodrow Wilson discovered that there were a number of other fundamental defects embedded in the Aldrich plan: 1) Membership in the National Reserve Association was voluntary, not mandatory. 2) Banks could continue to pyramid reserves at the National Reserve Association if they so desired. 3) In order to borrow reserves or acquire currency from the National Reserve Association in exchange for promissory notes as collateral, a bank had to get the concurrent approval of both the Governor of the National Reserve Association and the Treasury Secretary. 4) The National Reserve Association could issue new banknotes, redeemable in specie on demand, as its own obligation, not as an obligation of the U.S. government. It could issue these National Reserve banknotes at its sole discretion, in any quantity that it deemed prudent, and at any time of its own volition.

Membership in the Reserve Association had to be compulsory for all national banks in order for the U.S. to have a national elastic currency. The currency of the United States could never be truly elastic unless the country's reserves were centralized. Without being linked to a central bank, each of the nation's 7,500 independent national banks would separately place a quarter of its reserves in the bank's vault where the reserves would be of no use. The single national currency could be elastic only when the reserves of all national banks were pooled together in a central bank for the use of any member bank in its hour of need.

To prevent the problem of pyramiding of reserves, only commercial banks could be permitted to have bank accounts at the National Reserve; the members of the public or private businesses could not be allowed to open a bank account at the National Reserve. Pyramiding of reserves would then not be possible because the National Reserve, after accepting a deposit of reserves from a member bank, could not lend out those reserves to the public. Regarding the approval of both the Governor of the National Reserve Association and the Treasury Secretary that would be needed to borrow reserves or acquire currency, Verle B. Johnston writes in the weekly letter of January 6, 1984 of the Federal Reserve Bank of San Francisco on page 2:

"Another criticism of the Aldrich plan centered on the provision that required the approval of the Governor of the National Reserve Association and the concurrence of the Treasury Secretary when a bank used its own promissory note as collateral to acquire currency and borrow reserves from the Association. Critics argued that the geographical enormity of the U.S. and the highly diversified structure of its regional economies rendered such highly centralized control and decision making inappropriate. Similar objections were made to the proposal for a uniform nationwide discount rate."

To eliminate the possibility of a single national currency being issued at the sole discretion of the National Reserve Association, and also being printed as the sole obligation of the National Reserve Association, Treasury Secretary William G. McAdoo proposed a plan to create a 100% government owned central bank on May 20, 1912. This government owned bank, consisting of up to five reserve centers, would be under the jurisdiction and control of the Department of the Treasury, and would issue a single national currency to replace all other banknotes in circulation at that time. This national banknote, redeemable in specie, would be issued at the sole discretion of the Department of the Treasury, and would be an obligation of the United States government. William G. McAdoo was born in Marietta, Georgia during the Civil War, and he was married to Eleanor Randolph Wilson, the daughter of President Woodrow Wilson, in the White House on May 7, 1914.

President Woodrow Wilson is the only president in U.S. history with a Ph.D degree. He was the President of Princeton University before becoming Governor of New Jersey in 1910. Woodrow Wilson was born on December 28, 1856 in Staunton, Virginia and when he was only one year old, his family moved to Augusta, Georgia. As a young boy Woodrow Wilson would see Confederate army troops march into town, and would look on as his mother would carefully tend to the wounds of injured Union soldiers. In 1879, Wilson graduated from the College of New Jersey, which is now known as Princeton University. He passed the Georgia bar examination and started a law practice in Atlanta, Georgia in 1882. He gave up his life as a lawyer to enroll in the graduate program in history and political science in John Hopkins University in Baltimore where he was awarded a Ph.D degree in 1886. In 1890, he became a Professor of political Economy at Princeton, where after twelve years of teaching and research, he was appointed as the President of Princeton University in 1902. In the mid term elections of 1910, Wilson decisively defeated his Republican opponent to win the governorship of New Jersey. As a scholar, an academic, a politician, and as President, Dr. Woodrow Wilson now had to contend with three bills on monetary reform on his desk: the Glass Bill, the Owens Bill, and the McAdoo bill.

In March of 1912, the House Banking Committee formed a subcommittee under Representative Carter Glass, a Democrat from Virginia, whose first step as subcommittee chair was to hire the services of H. P. Willis to help produce an alternative to the Aldrich bill. Henry Parker Willis, a thirty seven year old professor at Washington and Lee University, taught economics and was a banking expert in his own right. Willis regularly took advice from James Laughlin, the University of Chicago economics professor, under whom he had studied banking and economics, as he proceeded to write a new banking bill for Representative Glass. The Glass bill that was eventually formulated was similar to the Aldrich plan in that it accepted the idea of central banking, and gave power and authority primarily to bankers, with very little say for the government. It differed from the Aldrich plan in that, instead of a single central body such as the National Reserve Association, the Glass plan envisaged a system of a minimum of twelve, or a maximum of twenty autonomous regional banks scattered throughout the United States. Membership in a regional reserve bank was mandatory for all national banks as opposed to voluntary membership in the Aldrich plan. Another major difference in the two plans was that the Glass plan required reserves to be placed in each of the regional reserve banks, whereas the Aldrich plan favored the centralization of reserves at the National Reserve Association. Author Roger Lowenstein writes in his book, America's Bank: The Epic Struggle to Create the Federal Reserve, on page 189:

"Of course, the plans also differed in important respects. The biggest was that Aldrich and Warburg had conceived of "branches" around the country subservient to a central organ. Glass was proposing regional "banks" with greater local independence - although arguably, this was a matter of degree. Another distinction was that Glass-Willis compelled the banks to shift their reserves to the new Reserve Banks, ending the perilous "pyramiding" of reserves from the farm to the city to New York. Aldrich, not wanting to offend his banker colleagues, had been mum on this important point".

In March of 1913, the Senate Banking and Currency Committee was created under the leadership of Senator Robert L. Owen, a Democrat of Oklahoma. Robert Latham Owen was partly of Cherokee descent from his mother's side, and he devoted many years of his life as the principal teacher of the Cherokee Orphan Asylum in Salina in what was then Indian Territory. He was appointed as the Federal Indian Agent in Muskogee for the so-called 'Five Civilized Tribes' in 1885. The Oklahoma and Indian Territories were consolidated to form the state of Oklahoma by the Oklahoma Enabling Act of 1907, and Owen was elected as one of the first of two Senators when Oklahoma was admitted to the Union in 1907.

Prior to finalizing his banking bill, Senator Owen had extensive discussions and consultations with Vanderlip, Warburg, and Piatt Andrews. In fact it was Professor A.P. Andrews who finally wrote the banking plan for Senator Owen. The Owen plan differed from the Glass plan in several important respects: 1) The Owen Plan mandated that the Federal Reserve notes should be issued by the federal government as government money, whereas the Glass plan wanted the notes to be issued by the Reserve

Banks as private money. 2) The Owen plan explicitly stated that all of the Federal Reserve Board members would be appointed by the President and confirmed by the Senate, whereas the Glass plan would allow some of the members to be appointed by bankers. 3) The Owen plan reduced the maximum number of regional reserve banks from twenty to twelve. 4) The Owen plan lowered the requirement for a member bank of the Federal Reserve System to subscribe to capital stock in the Federal Reserve Bank, from twenty percent to six percent of its combined capital and surplus, a change that was favorable for smaller banks.

The Glass bill was introduced in the House of Representatives as H.R. 7837 by democrat Carter Glass of Virginia on August 29, 1913, and it passed the House on September 18, 1913 by a vote of 287 to 85, with six Republicans joining every democrat. The Owen bill passed in the Senate on September 18, 1913 by a vote of 54 to 34, with three democrats voting against the bill. The Owen bill was passed after the Hitchcock bill was very narrowly defeated in the Senate by a margin of 43 against to 41 in favor of the bill. Senator Gilbert M. Hitchcock, a Democrat from Nebraska, had proposed a system of four reserve banks which would be controlled by the federal government at all levels, would issue government money, and whose stock would be sold to the public.

There were many differences between the Glass bill that passed in the House, and the Owen bill that passed in the Senate, and the final Owen-Glass bill emerged after these differences were reconciled in a conference committee which worked feverishly at a hectic pace, to bridge the gap between the two bills. It was agreed that there would be between eight and twelve Reserve Banks, with each Reserve Bank having a Governor and a nine person board of directors, and a seven member Federal Reserve Board of Governors, located in Washington D.C., to regulate and supervise the Federal Reserve Banks. The seven members of this Federal Reserve Board would be nominated by the President and confirmed by the Senate. All nationally chartered banks would be required to join the Federal Reserve System and had to contribute to the capital stock of the Reserve Bank System in an amount equal to six percent of the member bank's capital and surplus, and each member bank would receive a dividend of six percent. Each Reserve bank would have a nine-person board of directors including a Governor, with the Governors serving staggered terms of ten years each, so that no U.S. President could nominate all the governors of his choice during a two term presidency. National banknotes dating bank to the Lincoln era would be phased out, but other forms of currency such as greenbacks, silver certificates, gold coins, etc. would continue to serve as legal tender. It was agreed that the new Federal Reserve note would be an obligation of the U.S. Treasury, not of private banks, but Glass would not agree to give Federal Reserve notes the status of legal tender, although Federal Reserve notes eventually received the status of legal tender in 1933 by an act of Congress. Glass and his House conferees were also successful in removing deposit guarantee, and in not allowing member banks to include money in their bank vaults to count as reserves. The composition of the seven member Federal Reserve Board in the Senate version of the bill included the Treasury Secretary and six others; the House version of the bill included three government officials. In the end, both parties agreed to have only the Treasury Secretary and the Comptroller of the Currency with five other appointees on the Federal Reserve Board. After both the House and the Senate voted overwhelmingly in favor of the conference report on December 22 and December 23, respectively, President Woodrow Wilson signed the Owens-Glass bill into law as the Federal Reserve Act at 6 PM on December 23, 1913.

# THE FEDERAL RESERVE OPENS IN 1914

The Federal Reserve, with $203 million in gold in its vaults, opened for business on November 16, 2014 with twelve Reserve banks located in Atlanta, Boston, Chicago, Cleveland, Dallas, Kansas City, Minneapolis, New York, Philadelphia, Richmond, San Francisco, and St. Louis. The seven members of the Federal Reserve Board were Treasury Secretary William G. McAdoo, Comptroller of the Currency John Skelton, Assistant Treasury Secretary Charles S. Hamlin, investment banker Paul M. Warburg, Alabama banker William P.G. Harding, economist Adolph C. Miller of Berkeley, and Frederic A. Delano, uncle of Franklin D. Roosevelt.

After initially refusing the offer of a job as the Governor of the Federal Reserve Bank of New York at an annual salary of $30,000 per year, Benjamin Strong was subsequently persuaded by Henry Davison and Paul Warburg to accept the position. On October 5, 1914, the Federal Reserve Bank of New York, announced that Benjamin Strong would be the bank's first Governor.

A few months earlier war had broken out in Europe when, on Tuesday July 28, 2014, the Austro-Hungarian empire declared war on Serbia, following the assassination of Archduke Franz Ferdinand, heir to the throne of the Austro-Hungarian Empire, and his wife Sophie, by a Serb nationalist named Gavrilo Princip in Sarajevo, which is the present day capital of Bosnia Herzegovina. According to war historian John Keegan, in his book, The First World War, on pages 48 and 49:

"The Hapsburg army's summer manoeuvres of 1914 were held in Bosnia, the former Ottoman Turkish province occupied by Austria in 1878 and annexed to the empire in 1908. Franz Ferdinand, nephew to the Emperor Franz Joseph and Inspector General of the army, arrived in Bosnia on 25 June to supervise. After the manoeuvres concluded, on 27 June, he drove next morning with his wife to the provincial capital, Sarajevo, to carry out official engagements. It was an ill-chosen day: 28 June is the anniversary of the defeat of Serbia by the Turks in 1389, Vidov Dan, the event from which they date their long history of suffering at the hands of foreign oppressors. The role of oppressor, after the retreat of the Ottoman Turks, had been assumed, in the eyes of nationalist Serbs, by the Hapsburgs, and the provincial administration had been warned that his visit was unwelcome and might be dangerous." John Keegan continues on page 49:

"On the Archduke's way to the residence of the provincial governor, one of the terrorists threw a bomb at the car carrying Franz Ferdinand and his wife but it bounced off, exploding under the car following and wounding an officer occupant. The imperial party proceeded on its way. Three- quarters of an hour later, however, en route to visit the casualty in hospital, the archducal couple's chauffeur took a wrong turning and, while reversing, came to a momentary halt. The stop brought the car opposite one of the undetected conspirators, Gavrilo Princip, who was armed with a revolver. He stepped forward and fired. The Archduke's wife died instantly, he ten minutes later. Princip was arrested on the spot."

The same day that Austria-Hungary declared war on Serbia, the Dow dropped from 79 to 76, a four percent decline. Stocks fell by seven percent on Thursday July 30, 1914, the largest drop in a single day since the panic of 1907, when news arrived that Russia, in support of its ally Serbia, had ordered a general mobilization because of the bombardment of the Serbian capital of Belgrade by Austrian warships. At this time, foreign investors held a vast portfolio of about $6 billion worth of U.S. stocks and bonds, and even if only a fraction of these securities were sold off, U.S. reserves of gold would dwindle to zero. To forestall the liquidation of these foreign held securities, the New York Stock Exchange was closed on Friday July 31, 1914.

Germany began to mobilize and declared war on Russia on August 1,

1914, and in response, France and Belgium also started mobilizing. Two days later on August 3, 1914, Germany declared war on France, and invaded neutral Belgium which led to an ultimatum from Britain to Germany, calling on Germany to withdraw immediately from Belgium. Rejection of the British ultimatum by Germany resulted in a British declaration of war on Germany on August 4, 1914. All the major powers of Europe were now at war, and all of the major industrial combatants, Austria-Hungary, France, Germany, Russia, and Great Britain, suspended specie payments. In other words, these countries went off the gold standard.

On August 18, 1914, when the German army was in Brussels, only 200 miles away from Paris, the Banque de Paris had started moving its gold reserves of $800 million, weighing about 1,300 tons, to secret locations in Central and Southern France. When the Germans were only about 25 miles from Paris on August 29, 1914, the vaults at the Banque de Paris were empty. In September of 1914, The Reichsbank of Germany had about $500 million in gold reserves, but it had already taken the precaution of suspending the convertibility of the Mark into gold on July 31, 1914. In the first week of July of 1914, the Bank of England had approximately $200 million in reserves of gold, but when bullion reserves fell to $50 million on August 1, 1914, the Bank of England raised its interest rates to ten percent.

In August of 1914, the United States was the world's largest importer of capital, and U.S. businesses owed about $500 million to European creditors which would become due between August and December of 1914. With the outbreak of war, the world's financial markets were in disarray after acceptance houses and discount establishments in London started winding down their operations. It was possible that instead of rolling over the debt, European creditors might demand immediate repayment of the debt denominated in gold or pound sterling. This possibility forced U.S. holders of European debt to rush to exchange their dollars for the British pound, causing the exchange rate of the dollar to increase from $4.87 per pound to $7.65 per pound. According to Leland Crabbe, in the Federal Reserve Bulletin of June 1989 on page 424:

"Late in July, as foreigners began liquidating their holdings of U.S. securities and as U.S. debtors scrambled to meet their obligations to pay in sterling, the dollar-pound exchange rate soared as high as $6.75, far above the parity of $4.8665. Large quantities of gold began to flow out of the United States as the premium on sterling made exports of gold highly profitable. Under the pressure of heavy foreign selling, stock prices fell sharply in New York. The banking and financial systems in the United States seemed on the verge of collapse." Continuing on page 424:

"Although the international financial machinery broke down more fundamentally in 1914 than it had in previous crises, the U.S. domestic economy fared surprisingly well. Primarily because the issuance of emergency currency provided liquidity, the volume of loans made by banks was much higher than in past crises. Because banks in the country actually increased their loans outstanding, in contrast to their past practices, the crisis of 1914 did not unduly burden banks in New York. Although interest rates in the United States rose and remained high through the autumn, rates did not soar to the levels reached in past panics. By the time the Federal Reserve Banks opened, on November 16, 1914, the financial crisis in the United States had nearly passed. In November, commercial banks began to retire Aldrich-Vreeland notes. In December, gold began to flow toward the United States, and the New York Stock Exchange reopened. By January, with exports surging, the neutral dollar had rebounded to move past parity with the pound."

The Second World War proved to be a real bonanza for the United States, turning the country from the status of longtime debtor to that of net creditor. It was a windfall beyond imagination that swelled the gold stock of the nation from $1.57 billion in August of 1914 to $2.85 billion in April of 1917 (valued at $20.67 an ounce, according to the U.S. Bureau of the Census, Historical Statistics of the United States, Colonial Times to 1957, page 649). Exports of food, munitions, supplies, and other products, to the European combatants, sparked the onset of an enormous economic boom that resulted in a massive inflow of gold into the United States. These purchases of U.S. manufactured goods, in part funded by loans to Britain and France, fundamentally transformed the economic landscape and the international standing of the United States. U.S. investments abroad increased from $5 billion at the beginning of the war to $9.7 billion after the end of the war, while foreign investments in the U.S. declined from $7.2 billion to $3.3 billion during the same period. Instead of a debtor nation of $2.2 billion, the U.S. was now a creditor nation of $6.4 billion. The late Professor John Kenneth Galbraith of Harvard University, who served as U.S. Ambassador to India during the Kennedy administration from 1961 to 1963, had this to say in his book, Money Whence it Came, Where it Went, on page 137:

"Some of the gold came for deposit and safekeeping, some came to be invested in American securities, but the fundamental force in the flow was the need of the belligerent powers for American goods. In an age of socialist agriculture and Soviet wheat purchases, it requires an effort of mind to remember that Russia was once a major source of Europe's wheat. Now this market was cut off, and the United States became an important supplier of bread grain. Also needed were ships, armor plate and, above all, ammunition. By 1915, it was evident that the participants, Britain in particular, could never supply themselves with the infinity of shells which, according to the current concepts of warfare, had to be flung across no-man's-land before an offensive..." According to Galbraith on the next page, page 138 of the same book:

"Some of these supplies were paid for by conscripting and selling in the United States the American securities which earlier it had been thought their frightened owners would dump on their own. The spending of these proceeds involved no movement of gold. Some of the payment was from loans raised from private investors in the United States, which also occasioned no gold movement. In principle, it might be noted, these loans were available to both sides. In practice, the British controlled the oceans. Thus they made it impossible for their enemies to move any appreciable quantity of the products the loans would buy, so the Germans and Austrians had no need for the loans that this even-handed policy allowed. In consequence, William Jennings Bryan was led to the last of his many acts of public inconvenience. He held that such loans to the British were inconsistent with any neutrality that was strict, as Wilson had demanded, as to both thought and deed. For this aberration he was severely rebuked by those who believed that obvious truth should be subordinate to the demands of patriotism or the prospects of pecuniary gain. To the intense relief of such citizens, Bryan left the Cabinet in June 1915 over Wilson's reaction to the sinking of the Lusitania. He remains one of the tiny handful of Cabinet officers in the American experience to register opposition to a policy of which they disapproved by resigning."

The United States severed diplomatic relations with Germany after the

German Ambassador to the United States, Johann Von Bernstorff presented a note to U.S. Secretary of State Robert Lansing on January 31, 1917, indicating Germany's decision to resume unrestricted submarine attacks. The American freighter Housatonic, carrying 144,200 bushels of wheat for England, was stopped and then sunk by the German U-boat U-53, after releasing the crew unharmed, on February 3, 1917. Subsequently, after four more U.S. merchant ships were sunk by German U-boats by late March of 1917, President Wilson declared war on Germany on April 6, 1917, after both the Senate (82-6) and the House (373-50) had voted overwhelmingly in favor of war.

The fledgling Federal Reserve System was just getting organized when the massive inflow of European gold received as payment for exports to Britain and France, doubled the gold reserves of the U.S. between August of 1914 and April of 1917, which in turn increased the money supply and led to inflation rates of 12.5% in 1916, 19.66% in 1917, 17.86% in 1918, and 16.97% in 1919. The dollar of 1920 was worth only half that of the dollar of 1914. The young Federal Reserve System was powerless to control the expansion of the money supply or to check the concomitant high rates of price inflation during this period.

After the United States entered the first world war, the inflow of gold into the U.S. was halted, because now its allies Britain and France paid for their imports from the U.S. not in gold or securities, but with the proceeds of loans from the United States. During the period April 1917 to November 1920, the U.S. was very generous in advancing loans to its European allies. Britain received loans in the amount of $4.2 billion, France got loans of about $2.97 billion, and Italy was advanced loans totaling $1.63 billion. Where did the money for these loans come from?

There were three options available for raising money: taxation, borrowing, and printing money. During the Civil War, the government directly printed greenbacks, but in spite of adequate reserves of gold, the government did not need to directly print money during the first world war. The reason for this was that an indirect method was now available. The existence of the Federal Reserve System made it possible for the government to exchange its Treasury bonds at a Federal Reserve bank for Federal Reserve notes or deposits at its bank accounts at the Federal Reserve bank. Despite all the power and independence of the Fed, it has never been able to deny the Treasury's request to trade money for bonds in its entire operating history! If the government received money by selling its bonds to a commercial bank, the commercial bank would then trade those bonds with a Federal Reserve bank, and the commercial bank's account at the Federal Reserve bank would be credited with the amount of the purchase. Money is created either way; it makes no difference whether the Treasury directly sells bonds to a Federal Reserve bank or if it first sells the bonds to a commercial bank. Will money creation result if government securities are sold directly to the public? If an individual buys a Treasury bond with his own money, no money is created, but if a person borrows the money from a bank to buy government securities, then new money is certainly created.

Treasury Secretary William McAdoo launched an aggressive campaign to sell American war debt in the form of the so-called 'Liberty Bonds' to the public, and the Federal Reserve System was called upon to market the war debt to commercial banks and the public. The participation of the Federal Reserve banks was crucial to the efforts for raising funds for the war, because the Fed used its role as a central banker to the banking system to facilitate the sale of war debt. The U.S. Treasury was able to sell about $20 billion of war debt, about $10 billion of which was due to the efforts of the New York Federal Reserve Bank. Professional Investment Banker, Liaquat Ahamed writes in his book, Lords of Finance: The Bankers Who Broke The World, on pages 95-96:

"By the time the war drew to a close, the Fed was a transformed institution. While it was not completely immune from the pressure of war finance, unlike so many European central banks, it had resisted purchasing government bonds directly and only indirectly helped to fuel the expansion in money supply. It had therefore secured some credibility. More important, the war had irrevocably changed the economic and financial position of the United States in relation to the rest of the world. The Fed, which barely existed in 1914, now sat on the largest reservoir of gold bullion in the world, making it potentially the dominant player if and when the international gold standard was restored."

The first world war ended on the eleventh hour of the eleventh day of the eleventh month of 1918. The armistice was signed in the private railway carriage of French General Ferdinand Foch at Rethondes, a railroad station in the forest of Compiegne, about 50 miles northeast of Paris. The same railroad car was placed in the exact spot on June 21 of 1940 when Nazi leader Adolph Hitler accompanied by top Nazi officials Herman Goring, Wilhelm Keitel, and Joachim Von Ribbentrop arrived to witness the French sign an agreement that was essentially a French surrender. Adolph Hitler seated himself in the same seat that Ferdinand Foch sat in 1918. Foch's railway carriage was then taken to Berlin and put on display as a war trophy.

It took an additional six months of negotiations to finalize the peace treaty, known as the Treaty of Versailles, which was signed in the Hall of Mirrors at the palace of Versailles. The Treaty of Versailles imposed harsh territorial, economic, and military penalties on Germany in the form of dismemberment, occupation, disarmament, and reparations. Alsace Lorraine, which France had lost 40 years ago, would be returned to France; Eupen and Malmady would go to Belgium; North Schleswig would become part of Denmark after a plebiscite; Czechoslovakia received the Hultschin district; and Memel, a small strip of territory along the Baltic Sea, was given to Lithuania. Poland did not exist as an independent country during the first world war, but regained its independence as a sovereign nation in 1918 when it was reconstituted with territory taken from Germany, Russia, and Austria-Hungary. Silesia, Posen, and parts of West Prussia were taken from Germany to give Poland access to the Baltic Sea, which meant that East Prussia was cut off from the German mainland by a Polish corridor. The Rhineland was demilitarized and the industrial region of Saar was placed under the administration of the League of Nations. Germany lost 13% of its territory (27,000 square miles) and 10% of its population (between 6.5 and 7 million).

Article 231 of the Treaty of Versailles required that Germany compensate the victorious allies for the destruction it had caused to their people and property, but the amount of the reparations that Germany would have to pay was not specified in the treaty. A Reparations Commission based in Paris was set up to determine Germany's liability, and in the meantime, Germany needed to pay $5 billion no later than May 1, 1921. Louis-Lucien Klotz, the French Finance Minister, wanted to invoice Germany for 15 billion British pounds, to be paid in 34 annual installments of one billion pounds per year. However, the Reparations Commissions ultimately decided that Germany would have to pay war reparations in the amount of $35 billion, which is equivalent to about $512 billion in 2017 US dollars. Germany made the final payment of $95 million in 2010.

The issue of German reparations came under a scathing attack by none other than the foremost economist of the twentieth century, the late John Maynard Keynes, who received a first class honours degree in mathematics from Cambridge University and was placed second in the Civil Service Examination of 1906. Keynes studied briefly under Alfred Marshall, professor of economics at Cambridge University, but never got a degree in economics. According to economist and biographer Robert Skidelsky, in his introduction to 'The Essential Keynes' on page xviii:

"Keynes was chief Treasury representative at the Paris Peace Conference in 1919, where he tried unavailingly to limit Germany's bill for reparations, and to promote an American loan for the reconstruction of Europe. His resignation from the Treasury on 5 June 1919 was followed by the publication, in December, of The Economic Consequences of the Peace, the polemic, informed by both economic argument and moral passion, against Lloyd George's policy of trying to make Germany pay for the war 'till the pips squeak', it reflected his fears for the future of European civilization. Unless the Versailles Treaty were drastically revised, vengeance, he predicted, would follow."

'The Economic Consequences of the Peace' became an international bestseller, and after being translated into more than a dozen languages, it sold more than a hundred thousand copies in the first six months of its publication. Keynes explained in his book that in order for Germany to pay reparations to the Allies, it would first need to earn the money by exporting more than it was importing, that is, it would need to run a trade surplus. Who would absorb these massive amounts of German exports? It would surely disrupt world trade and cripple the industries of the importing countries. It was not realistic to expect Germany to pay $35 billion in reparations; he concluded that the maximum amount that Germany could possibly pay was two billion pounds.

While Germany owed reparations to the Allies, the Allies owed the huge amount of $12 billion in war debt to the United States, of which Britain owed $5 billion, and France owed $4 billion. During the Paris Peace Conference in April of 1919, British Prime Minister Lloyd

George forwarded to President Woodrow Wilson, a plan drafted by John Maynard Keynes, called the "Scheme for the Rehabilitation of European Credit and for Financing Relief and Reconstruction." This plan required Germany and other former central Powers to float a massive bond issue in the amount of 1,345,000,000 British pounds. Of this total amount of 1,345,000,000 pounds, Germany would issue bonds in the amount of 1,000,000,000 pounds, and give them to the allies as payment for war reparations. The Allies would then assign and hand these bonds over to the U.S. as payment for its war debt to the United States. According to the Keynes plan, these bonds were "to be accepted at their par value plus accrued interest in payment of all indebtedness between any of the Allied and Associated Governments." This would settle the debt question for all parties concerned. The Wilson administration rejected the Keynes Plan because it said the plan 'lacked financial soundness' in that the U.S. Treasury would find itself in possession of $5 billion worth of German bonds of questionable value, instead of bonds from more credit worthy foreign governments. In addition, payments on these bonds would actually be reparation payments, and President Wilson really did not like the idea of receiving German reparation payments. The British government also asked for a general cancellation of all war debt in February of 1920, something which the Wilson administration flatly refused to do.

After Warren J. Harding became President in March of 1921, his administration reiterated its position to the European Allies that there would be no cancellation of war debt. On February 9, 1922, the World War Foreign Debts Commission Act established a commission, under Treasury Secretary Andrew Mellon, to negotiate repayment plans with countries that had war debt. The War Debt Commission successfully negotiated 15 separate repayment plans with terms that depended upon the debtors' ability to pay. The principal amount of Allied debt was accepted as $11.5 billion, which was expected to yield $22 billion when paid in full after 62 years. Britain's debt was reduced by about 20% to $4.6 billion with interest set at 3% for the first ten years, and then 3.5% thereafter. France's war debt was reduced by half with no interest for the first five years, and then a gradual increase in the rate of interest to 3.5%. Within less than a year, the Germans defaulted on reparation payments, and consequently the Allies could not pay the U.S. This international problem was passed on to the administration of President Calvin Coolidge, who assumed the presidency, following the death of President Harding in August of 1923.

Before the first world war, Great Britain was the world's banker with over $20 billion in foreign investments. The city of London was the center of international banking and finance. But in order to finance four years of a terrible conflict, Britain had no choice but to liquidate most of its foreign investments and had to borrow vast sums of money from the United States. The first world war had shifted the financial balance of power from Great Britain to the United States.

# THE GREAT STOCK MARKET CRASH OF 1929

Incumbent President John Calvin Coolidge was reelected in the presidential election of 1924. During his term of office from August 3 of 1923, when he became President after the sudden death of President Harding, to March 4 of 1929 when Herbert Hoover was sworn in as President, the U.S. enjoyed a period of exceptional growth and prosperity. From 1923 to 1929, the nation's real income increased by 3.4% each year, and wholesale prices declined by an average of 0.9% per year. The Dow Jones Industrial Average more than quadrupled from 87.96 on August 1, 1923, to 381.17 on September 3, 1929, in concert with the unprecedented prosperity during this period. In what would subsequently go down in the annals of the stock market history of the United States for really bad timing, Yale economist and market pundit Professor Irving Fisher, told members of the Purchasing Agents Association at a monthly dinner meeting on Wednesday October 16, 1929, that "stock prices have reached what looks like a permanently high plateau."

Born in 1867, Irving Fisher earned his Ph.D from Yale, and almost died of tuberculosis in 1898. Fisher invented a machine for storing index cards, which was similar to but not exactly like a Rolodex, and sold the patent for this machine to Remington Rand for several million dollars in 1925. Fisher used the money that he received from Remington Rand to buy stocks on margin, and was worth an estimated $10 million in September of 1929. On Wednesday October 23, 1929, after 6,374,960 shares were traded on the NYSE, the DJIA declined from 326.51 to 305.85, a loss of 6.4%. On Thursday October 24, 1929, after 12,894,650 shares were traded, the stock market dropped from 305.85 to 299.47. The reason why the stock market fell by only 6.38 points on Black Thursday, October 24 is that after the stock market kept falling in the morning of that day, prominent bankers of investment banks decided in a meeting to pool their resources together, and support the market by buying large blocks of stock, which resulted in a rally in stock prices in the afternoon, thus offsetting the losses of the same morning. For the same reason, there was a moderate rally on Friday, October 25, 1929, when the stock market climbed to 301.22, after 5,923,220 shares had been traded. This small increase of 1.75 points was wiped out the next day, Saturday, October 25, 1929, when the DJIA fell to 298.97. The efforts of Wall Street Bankers, which included Charles E. Mitchell, the Chairman of the Board of the National City Bank, Albert H. Wiggins, the Chairman of the Chase National Bank, William C. Potter, the President of the Guaranty Trust Company, Seward Prosser, the Chairman of the Bankers Trust Company, and Thomas W. Lamont, the senior partner of Morgan's, to stabilize the stock market, and hence to thwart a possible stock market collapse were not successful, as the unfortunate events of the next two days were to prove.

The market went into a free fall on Black Monday, October 28, 1929. After 9,212,800 shares had been traded on this day, the stock market tumbled from 298.97 to 260.64, a loss of 13%, which wiped off $14 billion of the value of U.S. stocks. The stock market slump continued the next day, on Black Tuesday October 29, 1929, when the stock market fell from 260.64 to 230.07, an additional loss of 11.8%, after trading 16,410,030 shares of stock. Despite these losses in the Stock Market, Irving Fisher continued to insist that the stock market slide was only temporary, but again his prognostication proved to be utterly wrong because the Stock market eventually lost 90% of its value, to reach its bottom of 41.22 on July 8, 1932. Professor Irving Fisher lost his fortune and his house, living out his life supported by Yale University. It would take another 25 years for the Stock Market to recover from this great stock market crash - the Dow Jones Industrial Average would finally return to its former high of 381.17 on November 23, 1954.

Winston Churchill lost his position as Britain's Chancellor of the

Exchequer when the Conservative party lost the General Election, and a minority Labor government took over in June of 1929. He was on a visit to the United States with his son Randolph during the great crash, and chose to visit the NYSE on Black Tuesday, October 29. He was invited inside the NYSE and personally witnessed the scene inside the stock market on that fateful day. Churchill had invested heavily and recklessly in the NYSE at that time, and as a consequence of the stock market collapse of 1929, Churchill reportedly lost about $50,000, a sum that was equal to almost the entire amount of his life's savings at that time.

The United States had accumulated approximately 40% of the world's total reserves of gold by 1920, but after the Federal Reserve gradually reduced its discount rate, which is the rate of interest at which it lends to member banks, in three separate rate cuts to 3%, between April and August of 1924, gold began to flow from the U.S. to Europe. This flow of gold enabled Britain to return to the gold standard in 1925, and allowed France to increase its share of the world's gold reserve from 9% in 1927 to 17% in 1929. The Federal Reserve also carried out open market purchases, that is, it started buying government securities on the open market to increase the reserves of the banking system. This had the net effect of pushing down interest rates to record lows during the period of 1924 to 1927. In November of 1927, the stock market was booming, commodity prices were declining, and inflation was almost non existent.

But the Federal Reserve was concerned about the outflow of gold from the United States, and what it thought was excessive speculation in the stock market. The Federal Reserve felt that there was a big difference between 'productive' and 'speculative' uses of credit, and was worried about the increase in bank loans to brokers which was fueling the stock market boom. The Federal Reserve Board at that time erroneously believed that money used to buy stock was not available for productive use; in fact, when stocks are bought and sold, the funds with which stocks are purchased, do not vanish into oblivion, but only change hands from one person to another. Benjamin Strong died of tuberculosis in October of 1928, but during his tenure as the influential Governor of the Federal Reserve Bank of New York, he was against using monetary policy to curb speculation in the stock market. Even during the final few months of his life, Benjamin Strong argued that instead of tightening the money supply any further, the

Federal Reserve needed to leave the Stock Market alone and allow the stock market frenzy to subside on its own. However, in early 1928, flagrantly disregarding Strong's opinion, the Fed began to tighten its monetary policy by raising the discount rate from 3.5% in February of 1928 to 5% in July of 1928, in order to restrain speculation in stocks, and to stem the outflow of gold from the United States.

After his inauguration on March 4 of 1929, President Herbert Hoover continued to be critical of stock market speculation, especially the use of borrowed money to speculate in stocks, which he believed was an unproductive use of money. A few months later during President Hoover's presidency, the discount rate was increased by the Federal Reserve from five percent to six percent on August 8, 1929. In their book, A Monetary History of the United States, Milton Friedman and Anna J. Schwartz, noted on page 289 that:

"By July, the discount rate had been raised in New York to 5%, the highest since 1921, and the system's holdings of government securities had been reduced to a level of over $600 million at the end of 1927 to $210 million by August 1928, despite an outflow of gold." Friedman and Schwartz then wrote that, "During the two months from the cyclical peak in August 1929 to the crash, production, wholesale prices, and personal income fell at annual rates of 20 per cent, 7-1/2 per cent, and 5 per cent, respectively."

# THE GREAT DEPRESSION

Benjamin Strong was recovering from ill health in mid 1927, and so instead of traveling to Europe as he normally did in previous years, he decided to invite Montagu Norman, Governor of the Bank of England, Hjalmar Schacht, the Head of the Reichsbank, and Emile Moreau, Governor of the Banque de Paris, to come to New York for a meeting. Moreau did not speak English, and therefore chose to send Charles Rist, the Deputy Governor of the Banque de Paris to represent him at the meeting. The Banco d'Italia expected an invitation also, but was not invited by Strong.

Norman and Schacht arrived in New York on the Mauretania in great secrecy on July 1, 1927, and was joined by Charles Rist, who had arrived in New York two days earlier, to join the conference with Benjamin Strong at the New York Fed. At the meeting, Norman asked Strong for help with Britain's precarious reserve position. If the U.S. would lower its interest rate, then gold would flow to Britain because of the higher return in Britain, and the competitive position of British industry and labor would be considerably improved. As a result of this meeting, the Federal Reserve reduced the rate of interest from 4 per cent to 3.5 per cent in August 1927. After this interest rate cut went into effect, the DJIA went up from 184.21 on 8/1/1927 to 202.4 on 12/31/1927. Loans to brokers for carrying securities on margin also increased during this period.

Adolph C. Miller, a member of the Federal Reserve Board, and Herbert Hoover, the Secretary of Commerce in the Coolidge administration, were both adamantly opposed to this interest rate cut initiated by Benjamin Strong, and compelled the Federal Reserve to reverse course. After only six months, the Fed raised the discount rate gradually from 3.5% in February of 1928, to 5% in July of 1928, and then from 5% to 6% in August of 1929.

The interest rate cut of only 0.5% from 4% to 3.5% in August of 1927 which was in effect for only about six months until it was reversed in February of 1928, has been blamed as an error on the part of the Federal Reserve because it set in motion a train of events that led to the stock market crash of October 1929. This interest rate cut generated additional liquidity which could not be absorbed by the weak economy for real production at that time. The additional liquidity found its way into financial markets to fund the stock market boom that preceded the stock market crash.

According to many scholars, including Milton Friedman and Anna J. Schwartz, the Fed again made another error in tightening the money supply by raising the discount rate from 5% to 6% in August of 1929. This interest rate increase had unforeseen ramifications in that foreign central banks on the gold standard were compelled to raise their own interest rates. This pushed many foreign economies into recession, causing international commerce to contract, and the international economy to slow. There was no appropriate response from the Fed just after the crash in October of 1929. In fact, immediately after the crash, the Fed did not act in a decisive manner. According to William Greider, in his book, Secrets of the Temple, on page 299:

"Money disappeared on a massive scale. As billions of dollars of bank debt were liquidated by defaults and bankruptcies in the economy, involving farmers and businesses along with the stock-market speculators, the process naturally extinguished money and the supply of money contracted. From 1929 to early 1933, U.S. money shrank in volume by more than one-third. The Federal Reserve could have intervened to reverse the contraction. It could have reduced interest rates sharply to stimulate renewed borrowing and business activity. More importantly, it could have purchased millions or billions in government securities - pumping new money into the banking system to reverse the price deflation and restart the dead economy. Instead, as President Herbert Hoover lamented, the Fed became a 'a week reed for a nation to lean on in time of trouble'."

The crash frightened the people of the United States, many of whom lost their life savings. People were afraid of losing their jobs, and were uncertain about their ability to pay their bills in future. The immediate impact of the crash was to deepen the recession that had begun in the summer of 1929, but no one could imagine that this was only the beginning of what would be the longest and deepest depression in the history of the United States.

The Federal Reserve Banks did reduce the interest rate, in the months following the crash, in increments of 0.5 per cent, from 6 per cent in November of 1929, to 1.5 per cent in 1931. But this was a very slow and lethargic response to the massive reductions in output, employment, and prices that were taking place during this period. After Britain's suspension of the gold standard on September 21, 1931, the Fed decided to reverse gears, and increased the interest rate from 1.5% to 2.5% on October 8, 1931, and then from 2.5% to 3.5%, one month later. The results were catastrophic; the monetary base contracted by an additional $90 million, and there was a drastic fall in industrial production of another twenty five per cent within the next six months.

In October of 1929, industrial production was down by five per cent, and in the following month of November 1929, industrial production was down by an additional five percent. Unemployment doubled from 1.5 million in mid 1929 to about 3 million in early 1930. Consumer demand for big ticket items that people purchased on credit, like automobiles, radios, and refrigerators fell sharply, with car registrations throughout the U.S. falling by 25%. As demand declined, firms slashed production and laid off workers, causing unemployment to rise.

The U.S. GDP did record an overall growth of 5% for the entire year of 1929, that is for the period from January 1, 1929 to December 31, 1929, but it must be noted that the U.S. economy had slowed considerably by mid 1929, and was in recession just before the crash. After the great crash occurred in October of 1929, the recession worsened, but a recovery was expected within a year. The U.S. was poised for an economic rebound in the fall of 1930, when a series of bank panics beginning in November of 1930, transformed a typical recession into the beginning of the Great Depression.

In November 1930, approximately 8,000 commercial banks were members of the Federal Reserve System, but almost 16,000 banks were not members. These non member banks conducted their day to day banking activities in an environment that was fraught with the danger of bank panics. Non member banks held some of their reserves in their own vaults, but most of their reserves were in correspondent banks, only some of whom were members of the Federal Reserve System. In practice this meant that a country bank might not be able to access its reserves if the correspondent bank did not have reserves available if and when the country bank was in need of its reserves. In a situation where a respondent bank in need of reserves was not able to get its reserves from a correspondent bank, there was the distinct possibility of a depositor run.

Caldwell and Company, the largest financial holding company in the South, lost vast amounts of money in the stock market crash of 1929. To cover its losses, the company drained cash from subsidiary banks that it owned. The Bank of Tennessee, a Caldwell subsidiary, closed on November 7, 1930. Two more Caldwell subsidiaries in Knoxville, Tennessee, and Louisville, Kentucky, were shut down on November 12, and November 17, of 1930, respectively. These bank failures sparked bank runs that compelled hundreds of correspondent banks to halt operations, most of whom were eventually liquidated. Bank panic again erupted when the Bank of United States was shut down on December 11, 1930. Similarly, in June of 1931, networks of non member banks in Chicago were faced with depositor runs because these banks had invested in assets, primarily in real estate, that had lost value.

The banking crises of 1930-31 greatly accelerated the economic collapse, and subsequently, the economy declined in each of the years 1930, 1931, 1932, and 1933. The United States GDP which was $91.2 billion in 1930, plummeted to $56.4 billion in 1933, a contraction of 38.4% over the four year period. The Consumer Price Index, which was 71.4 in 1930, fell to 55.4 in 1933, reflecting prices that fell 22.4%, that is, a deflation of 22.4% during this period. The money supply of M1, which is currency plus demand deposits, shrank from $25.8 billion in 1930 to $19.9 billion in 1933, a shrinkage of 22.9% in four years. There were a total of 25,568 commercial banks in 1929, but only 14,771 banks remained in 1933, after 10,797 banks failed, a bank liquidation rate of 42.3% during this five year period. There were 1.55 million unemployed out of a labor force of 49.44 million in 1929, compared to the 12.83 million unemployed out of a labor force of 51.84 million in 1933. The unemployment rate had increased from 3.14% in 1929 to 24.75% in 1933.

During this economic crisis which was destroying the economy of the United States, the governor of New York, Democrat Franklin D. Roosevelt, won the presidential election of November 8, 1932 in a landslide, defeating incumbent President Herbert Hoover by 472 to 59 electoral votes, and 21,821,857 to 15,761,841 popular votes. Franklin D. Roosevelt was inaugurated as the 32$^{nd}$ President of the United States on Saturday March 4, 1933, and thirty six hours after he was sworn in as President, at 1:00 AM on Monday, March 6, 1933, President Roosevelt declared a four day nationwide bank holiday, which immediately closed all banks in the United States, including the Federal Reserve.

According to Proclamation 2039, "no such banking institution or branch shall pay out, export, earmark, or permit the withdrawal or transfer in any manner or by any device whatsoever, of any gold or silver coin or bullion or currency or take any other action which might facilitate the hoarding thereof; nor shall any such banking institution or branch pay out deposits, make loans or discounts, deal in foreign exchange, transfer credits from the United States to any place abroad, or transact any other banking business."

The legislation called the Emergency Banking Act of 1933, had already been prepared earlier by the staff of the Department of the Treasury during the Hoover administration, and after it was introduced on March 9 of 1933, Congress voted in its favor the same evening, confirming the powers assumed by the President in declaring the bank holiday, and authorizing emergency issues of Federal Reserve Notes backed by any assets of a commercial bank. Title III of this act permitted the Secretary of the Treasury to ascertain if a bank needed additional funds to stay in business, and with the approval of the President to authorize the Reconstruction Finance Corporation to invest in the preferred stock of commercial banks, or to make loans secured by such stock as collateral. In his fireside chat of March 12, 1933, President Roosevelt told the American public:

"By the afternoon of March 3, scarcely a bank in the country was open to do business. Proclamations temporarily closing them in whole or in part had been issued by the Governors in almost all the States. It was then that I issued the proclamation providing for the nation-wide bank holiday, and this was the first step in the Government's reconstruction of our financial and economic fabric. The second step was the legislation promptly and patriotically passed by the Congress confirming my proclamation and broadening my powers so that it became possible in view of the requirement of time to extend the holiday and lift the ban of that holiday gradually. This law also gave authority to develop a program of rehabilitation of our banking facilities. I want to tell our citizens in every part of the Nation that the national Congress - Republicans and Democrats alike - showed by this action a devotion to public welfare and a realization of the emergency and the necessity for speed that is difficult to match in our history."

Like John Maynard Keynes who viewed gold as a 'barbarous relic', Professor Irving Fisher was steadfast in his conviction that the United States needed to go off the gold standard in order to end debt deflation. Although his prestige as an economist had fallen because of his incorrect prediction about the stock market, he still continued to offer his advice, for what it was worth, to incoming President Franklin D. Roosevelt during the transitional period of four months between election day and inauguration day. Irving Fisher repeatedly urged President Roosevelt to abandon the gold standard immediately.

The combination of Titles I and IV of the 1933 Emergency Banking Act of 1933, effectively removed the United States and Federal Reserve Notes from the strictures of the gold standard as soon as the law was enacted on March 9, 1933. Title I of the law established a new framework for designing monetary policy by giving the President the power and authority to conduct monetary policy independently, without approval from the Federal Reserve System.

On April 5, 1933, President Roosevelt ordered all gold coins and gold certificates to be redeemed for Federal Reserve notes. Individuals in the U.S. were asked to bring all gold coin, gold bullion, and gold certificates owned by them to the Federal Reserve by May 1 to exchange for paper currency at the set price of $20.67 per ounce of gold. After the United States went off the gold standard when the Emergency Banking Act was enacted, President Roosevelt formally suspended the gold standard on April 20, 1933, with a proclamation that enjoined the export of gold, and prohibited the Treasury or any financial institution from exchanging banknotes or demand deposits for gold coins or ingots. Six weeks later on June 5, 1933, a joint resolution of Congress abrogated the gold clauses in private and public obligations that required a debtor to repay the creditor in gold of the same weight and fineness as those borrowed, or in gold's monetary equivalent, at the value set in 1900. The United States Supreme Court upheld the constitutionality of these actions in a series of cases that it agreed to hear on this matter.

The next phase of President Roosevelt's gold program started with his gold purchase plan in October of 1933. During this phase, the Roosevelt administration instructed the Reconstruction Finance Corporation to purchase gold at higher prices, which in essence constituted a devaluation of the dollar on purpose. The dollar's worth in terms of an ounce of gold declined, whereas an ounce of gold was worth more in terms of dollars. Lowering the value of the dollar in terms of gold also lowered the value of the dollar in relation to foreign currencies. Hence U.S. commodities and manufactured goods became cheaper abroad, thus boosting U.S. exports. Conversely, the devaluation of the dollar made foreign products more expensive, thus reducing imports into the United States.

For the next three months, the Roosevelt administration gradually kept raising the price of gold until in January of 1934, President Roosevelt decided to stabilize the price of gold at $35 per ounce. From $20.67 an ounce in the spring of 1933, the price of gold was gradually raised to $35 an ounce by January of 1934, causing a 69 per cent devaluation of the dollar. In U.S. dollars, the value of the gold being held as reserves on the Federal Reserve's balance sheet, also increased simultaneously by 69 per cent.

President Roosevelt's gold program culminated in the Gold Reserve Act of January 30, 1934 which transferred ownership of all gold and gold certificates in the U.S. to the United States Treasury. Gold coins and bullion in possession of individuals and institutions, including the Federal Reserve System, needed to be surrendered to the U.S. Treasury in exchange for paper dollars at the exchange rate of $35 per ounce of gold. The U.S. Treasury then stored this gold in the United States Bullion Depository in Fort Knox near Louisville, Kentucky, and in other locations. The nationalization of gold in the United States by December 28, 1933, gave the U.S. Treasury a windfall of $2.81 billion because it acquired gold at $20.67 before the price of gold was raised to $35 per ounce. This $2.81 billion windfall was used by the Treasury to create an Exchange Stabilization Fund with which the Treasury could buy or sell gold, foreign currencies, financial securities, and other financial instruments in order to stabilize the exchange rate of the dollar against foreign currencies, without the help or approval of the Federal Reserve.

Before the Gold Reserve Act, citizens could exchange paper currency for gold and vice versa, whenever they wished to do so. After the Gold Reserve Act, it was possible to convert gold into paper currency but paper currency could not be exchanged for gold. Although the United States had abandoned the gold standard, it should be noted that from January 31, 1934 to August 15, 1971, the United States Treasury continued to sell gold only to foreign monetary authorities and licensed industrial users at $35 per ounce. This price of gold pegged at $35 per ounce would remain in effect until August 15, 1971, the day when President Nixon would announce a unilateral U.S. suspension of the convertibility of dollars into gold. According to the Bretton Woods agreement of 1944, foreign governments and central banks could exchange US dollars for gold at $35 per ounce. After Nixon's resignation in 1975, his successor President Gerald Ford would sign legislation in 1974 that would again permit the citizens of the United States to own gold.

The change in the nominal price of gold from $20.67 to $35 per ounce served as a powerful incentive to foreign exporters of gold to the United States. The higher price of gold acted as a spur to the world's gold mining industry, and consequently a higher volume of gold production added about $1 billion to the world's gold reserves. From 1933 to 1937, the reserves of gold at the Federal Reserve and the U.S. Treasury tripled from $4 billion to $12 billion. During the same period, the GDP grew at an average rate of 8%, while the money supply M1, expanded by 10% each year, as a result of the inflow of gold, and the flight of capital to the United States. The amount of gold in the U.S. Treasury increased from 6,358 metric tonnes in 1930 to 8,998 metric tonnes in 1935, and then to 19,543 metric tonnes in 1940.

The Federal Reserve System was restructured by the Banking Act of 1935 which was signed by President Roosevelt on August 23, 1935. The federal deposit insurance corporation that was created on a temporary basis on June 6 of 1933, was made permanent by Title I of this act. The FDIC would insure all accounts upto $5,000, all member banks of the Federal Reserve System would be required to participate, and the Board of Directors would include the Comptroller of the Currency, and two other members selected by the President and confirmed by the Senate. Title II of this act changed the name of the "Federal Reserve Board" to the "Board of Governors of the Federal Reserve System." The Head of the Board of Governors was now called the Chairman of the Board of Governors. All members of the Board, previously called members, received the title of Governor. The Board would consist of seven members selected by the President with the consent of the Senate. A Federal Open Market Committee (FOMC) consisting of twelve members would include all seven members of the Board of Governors, the President of the Reserve Bank of New York, and the Presidents of four other Reserve Banks on a rotating basis. Control of open market operations was given to the FOMC, where voting rules favored the Board of Governors. The participation of Reserve Banks in open market operations, that is, the buying and selling of securities on the open market, would be controlled by the FOMC. Reserve requirements and interest rates for deposits at member banks would also be set by the Board of Governors.

Title II of the Banking Act of 1935 altered the structure, powers, and functions of the Federal Reserve System. There was a significant shift in the locus of control from private hands to public hands in the Federal Reserve System, because this Act transferred power from the regional reserve banks, whose control lay in private hands, to the Board of Governors in Washington DC, where control resided in the hands of publicly appointed members. The relationship between the Federal Reserve System and the legislative branch, which happens to be Congress, was clearly delineated. At the same time, the relationship between the Federal Reserve and the executive branch, which consists of the President and his Cabinet, the various departments, and the many agencies of the government, was made unambiguous. By clarifying these relationships, the Federal Reserve System's leadership structure became more transparent.

Since the Federal Reserve Act of 1913, the Federal Reserve Board always had two ex officio members. Two members of the executive branch, the Treasury Secretary and the Comptroller of the Currency, were always automatic members of the Federal Reserve Board, but their services were no longer required on the Federal Reserve Board after the Banking Act of 1935 went into effect. When the Federal Reserve first opened in 1914, each of the twelve regional Federal Reserve Banks conducted open market operations in its own district, and made their own decision regarding the choice, quantity, and price of the securities that they intended to purchase. These independent, isolated, and rather uncoordinated purchases of securities by a Reserve Bank in one district, affected the market for securities in other districts. To address this problem, the Reserve Banks of New York, Boston, Chicago, Cleveland, and Philadelphia, formed a committee in 1922 to act in concert, and jointly engage in open market operations. This kind of cooperation among Federal Reserve Banks broke down in 1933 during the great depression, and Congress responded with the Glass-Steagall Act of 1933, in which the Federal Open Market Committee (FOMC) was created. The FOMC was comprised of twelve Governors, one from each of the twelve Federal Reserve Banks, and their decisions regarding open market operations were final and binding on all reserve banks. The Banking Act of 1935 altered this organizational arrangement of the FOMC by requiring a board consisting of seven Governors from the Board of Governors, the President of the Federal Reserve Board of New York, and the presidents from four of the other eleven Federal Reserve banks, on a rotational basis.

Marriner S. Eccles was employed as an assistant to the Treasury Secretary Henry Morgenthau when President Roosevelt appointed him to be the Chairman of the Federal Reserve Board on November 15, 1934. He was the architect of the banking Act of 1935, and when Congress invited him to present his analysis of the Great Depression, many of the ideas that he articulated in that Senate hearing in 1933, later became the basis of President Roosevelt's New Deal program. According to William Greider in his book, Secrets of the Temple: How the Federal Reserve Runs the Country, on page 309:

"When Marriner Eccles testified before a Senate hearing in early 1933, he found a receptive audience. In addition to the new economic principles, Eccles described a specific agenda for how the federal government could spend more money: unemployment relief, public works, agricultural allotments, farm mortgage refinancing and settlement of foreign war debts. He also proposed reforms for long-term stability: federal insurance for bank deposits, a centralized Federal Reserve System, tax reform to redistribute income, a minimum-wage law, unemployment insurance, old-age pensions, federal regulation of the stock market and other economic sectors. In one sitting, a Mormon Republican banker from Utah had described most all of the reforms that would become known as the New Deal agenda of Franklin Delano Roosevelt."

# THE CHICAGO PLAN

The winner of the 1921 Nobel Prize in Chemistry, Frederick Soddy of the United Kingdom, presented the conceptual framework of the Chicago Plan in his book, Wealth, Virtual Wealth, and Debt, published in 1926. Based on some of Soddy's original ideas in this 1926 book, The Chicago Plan was a six page memorandum of a monetary reform proposal, drafted in March of 1933 by a group of economists at the University of Chicago, which was given limited and confidential distribution to about forty individuals on March 16, 1933. Henry A. Wallace, the Secretary of Agriculture in the Roosevelt administration, received a copy of the memorandum with a cover letter signed by Frank H. Knight, a Professor at the University of Chicago.

In 1927, Dr. Frank H. Knight, who was at that time a Professor at the University of Iowa, published a review of Frederick Soddy's 1926 book, Wealth, Virtual Wealth, and Debt, in the Saturday Review of Literature dated April 16, 1927. Although Professor Knight was critical of some aspects of Soddy's book, he was nonetheless impressed by the practical thesis of the book, and wrote on page 732:

"The practical thesis of the book is distinctly unorthodox, but in our opinion both highly significant and theoretically correct. In the abstract, it is absurd and monstrous for society to pay the commercial banking system "interest" for multiplying several fold the quantity of medium of exchange when (a) a public agency could do it at negligible cost, (b) there is no sense in having it done at all, since the effect is simply to raise the price level, and (c) important evils result, notably the frightful instability of the whole economic system and its periodical collapse in crises, which are in large measure bound up with the variability and uncertainty of the credit structure if not directly the effect of it." Professor Knight concluded his review by praising the book in the following manner:

"The concepts of wealth, virtual wealth (money), and debt emphasize important and neglected distinctions, and in general it is a brilliantly written and brilliantly suggestive and stimulating book."

Six years later, as a Professor at the University of Chicago, Frank H. Knight, and his colleague at the University of Chicago, Professor Henry Simons, were the principal authors of the confidential six page memorandum on monetary reform, that came to be known as the 'Chicago Plan', and was submitted to President Roosevelt's Secretary of Agriculture, Henry A. Wallace on March 16, 1933. The monetary reform proposal was supported by prominent economists from other universities such as Paul H. Douglas of the University of California, Irving Fisher of Yale, Willford I. King of NYU, Charles R. Whittesley of Princeton, Earl J. Hamilton of Duke, Frank D. Graham of Princeton, and many others.

The fundamental feature of the Chicago Plan was that it would abolish money creation based on fractional reserves, the mechanism by which private banks are able to create money by making loans based on fractional reserves, and replace this debt based money with debt free money issued by the government for payment of all debts, private and public. Money creation would be separated from money lending because the power to issue currency would belong only to the government, while private commercial banks would only make loans with preexisting money, that is, they would make loans based on 100% reserves of money that the government had already created. Private commercial banks would have to maintain 100% reserves on checking accounts, which means that a bank would have to hold a dollar in reserve for every dollar of a depositor's balance in a checking account. Money deposited in savings accounts could be lent, but no more than the total amount collected as deposits in savings accounts, because banks would no longer be able to loan money into existence, based on fractional reserve banking. Private banks would merely become service providers of preexisting money, by holding demand deposits in checking accounts for customers, and by taking in deposits for savings accounts from savers, for lending those savings deposits of money based on 100% reserves.

Henry Simons wrote a revised version of the Chicago Plan in November 1933, after many comments and suggestions were received on the original plan between March and November of 1933. This version consisted of thirteen pages, and was signed by the same group of economists as in the original plan of March 1933. This version of the Chicago Plan required the outright abolition of fractional reserve banking, government ownership of Federal Reserve Banks, enhanced Congressional authority to charter banks for deposit banking, establishment of deposit banks with 100% reserves consisting of notes and deposits at Federal Reserve Banks, elimination of reserve requirements for Federal Reserve Banks, and making the Federal Reserve Note the only legal paper currency in the country.

President Roosevelt informed Congress in January 1934 that legislation was needed to reform the currency system, and also to make the U.S. government the sole proprietor of all monetary gold reserves. This message from President Roosevelt to Congress prompted the Chicago group of economists to engage in a push to draft legislation necessary to transform the Chicago Plan for banking reform into law.

The Roosevelt administration was in regular contact with the Chicago economists and Irving Fisher, and gave serious consideration to the Chicago Plan, as evidenced by the government memoranda of Gardiner Means in 1933 and Lauchlin Currie in 1934. Republican Bronson Cutting from New Mexico was reelected to the Senate after very narrowly defeating Democrat Dennis Chavez with 76,226 votes in his favor, to Chavez's 74,944 votes. Cutting crossed party lines to support FDR in the 1932 presidential elections, and was an ardent supporter of the Chicago Plan. In December 1933, Senator Cutting received a copy of the November 1933 version of the Chicago Plan, which was mailed to him by Robert M. Hutchins, the President of the University of Chicago. In response, Senator Cutting asked Hutchins to draft a bill for the Chicago Plan.

After not hearing from Hutchins for several months, Cutting sent a telegram to Hutchins on March 7, 1934 asking him about the Chicago Plan Bill. As a result, Henry Simons journeyed to Washington DC to personally meet Senator Cutting in order to discuss the important aspects of the contemplated bill. Henry Simons felt that he was not qualified to write a bill, and hence presented only an outline of the bill to Senator Cutting and Senator Robert La Follette, Jr. The actual bill for the Chicago Plan was drafted by Robert H. Hemphill, a newspaper writer. Senator Cutting introduced bill S 3744 in the Senate on June 6, 1934, and Congressman Wright Patman introduced it in the House as HR 9855, but the bill failed to pass in Congress.

On May 6, 1935, Senator Cutting perished in a fatal plane crash in Missouri when he was returning from Albuquerque to Washington DC in a Transcontinental & Western Air DC-2. Senator Cutting had gone to New Mexico to collect evidence to refute Democrat Dennis Chavez's charge that Cutting's victory by 1,282 votes was rigged. In a special election in 1936, Chavez won the vacant Senate seat for New Mexico, and was subsequently reelected four more times. He served as a Senator until his death in 1962. Senator Cutting's untimely death dealt a mortal blow to any remaining chance for the passage of a Chicago Plan bill. Instead, fierce and unrelenting pressure from the banking lobby resulted in the Banking Act of 1935 which President Roosevelt signed into law on August 23, 1935.

According to Bernard Lietaer, Christian Arnsperger, Sally Goerner, and Stefan Brunnhuber, in their book, Money and Sustainability: The Missing Link, on pages 130 and 131:

"While we appreciate the strengths of the idea of nationalising the monetary creation process, there are five reasons why we do not recommend this solution.

1.  Replacing a monoculture with another monoculture is not the way to generate diversity in exchange media. As was shown in Chapter IV, any monoculture leads to a structural instability. Replacing a private monopoly with a public one wouldn't resolve the problem of structural fragility.

2.  While it is true that a 'Chicago Plan' reform would eliminate the risk of widespread banking crashes and of sovereign debt crises, there would still be monetary crises. In other words, as was shown in Chapter III, the 145 banking crises and 76 sovereign-debt crises that have hit the world since 1970 would have been avoided if such a reform had been in place. The 208 monetary crashes would not necessarily have been avoided.

3.  If governments were the only ones in charge of creating money, there might be a risk of inflation rising to a greater extent than it

has in the past. Such a risk is real and most recently demonstrated in 2009 by the hyperinflation crippling the Zimbabwean dollar after President Mugabe instructed the central bank to print its currency by the trillions.

4.  The fourth reason can be summarised as 'political realism'. Any version of the Chicago Plan will be fought to the death by the banking system because it threatens both its power base and its business model. Even after the excesses triggering the 2007-2008 collapse, or in the middle of the Great Depression of the 1930s, the banking lobby managed to deflect the implementation of any significant changes. Recall that in 2010, for every electoral official in Washington, there were three high-level lobbyists working full-time for the banking system. Thomas Freidman writes in the New York Times: "Our Congress today is a forum for legalised bribery. One consumer group using information from Opensecrets.org calculates that the financial services industry, including real estate, spent $2.3 billion on federal campaign contributions from 1990 to 2010, which was more than the health care, energy, defence, agriculture and transportation industries combined. Why are there 61 members on the House Committee on Financial Services? So many congressmen want to be in a position to sell votes to Wall Street." In Europe, there is no awareness of this problem because no legislation is in place requiring lobbyists to register at the European level. What are the chances of something as radical as the Chicago Plan being implemented when legislators themselves are part of an army of bank lobbyists?

5.  The final argument is about risk. Nationalising the money creation process cannot be done on a small pilot scale. It must be implemented on a massive national scale or, in the case of the euro, a multinational scale. Any change always involves the risk of unintended consequences. Logically, large-scale change involves greater risk. It is certainly a higher risk than any of the options presented in the next chapters."

For the above reasons so cogently articulated by Bernard Lietaer et al., the nationalization of the Federal Reserve System is not a panacea that will end the possibility of future monetary problems, nor is the establishment of public banks a solution to ameliorate the deficiencies of the private banking system. The revised version of the Chicago Plan written in 1939 entitled, 'A Program For Monetary Reform' would have been adequate 78 years ago, but it is not adequate at present to reform the monetary system as it exists in 2017. Despite dramatic advances in technology during the last eighty years, the monetary system of the United States has not been modernized since the Banking Act of 1935 was signed into law by President Roosevelt.

# THE US DOLLAR AS THE WORLD'S RESERVE CURRENCY

For the purpose of modernizing the United States monetary system, the first step that must be taken, a step that is absolutely essential, is the inevitable creation of an electronic currency that is totally cashless. This electronic currency must exist digitally only as numbers in a computer, and must not exist in the form of cash. We cannot arrive at this totally electronic currency by demonetizing all Federal Reserve Notes, that is, it is not possible to eliminate the existence of the U.S. dollar in the form of physical cash. Why is this so?

For all practical purposes it is not possible to eliminate the paper currency of the United States which exists in the form of Federal Reserve Notes, because of the simple reason that the United States dollar happens to be the world's reserve currency. Since 1945 the U.S. dollar has played a central role in facilitating international exchange for both the private and government sectors. The U.S. dollar performs as medium of exchange, store of value, unit of account, and standard of deferred payment.

As a medium of exchange, the U.S. dollar is used all over the world so extensively as a form of cash currency, that it is estimated that about $580 billion, or around 65% of all U.S. physical paper currency notes, were in circulation outside the territory of the United States in 2009. This includes 74% of $100 bills, 56% of $50 bills, and 58% of $20 bills. Some countries have adopted the U.S. dollar as their own currency such as Ecuador, El

Salvador, Zimbabwe, East Timor, Palau, Micronesia, Turks and Caicos, Marshall Islands, and the British Virgin Islands.

The foreign demand for U.S. banknotes results in a significant amount of seigniorage for the United States. Seigniorage is derived from the word 'seigneur' which refers to a medieval lord who had the right to keep some of the metal from which gold coins were minted. It costs only a few cents for the Bureau of Engraving and Printing to print a $100 bill, but a foreign country or business has to provide real goods or services worth $100 to be able to acquire this $100 bill. Foreign countries had to provide real goods and services to the United States in the amount of $580 billion to receive paper currency in the sum of $580 billion which they are holding. The U.S. paper currency that foreigners are holding can be thought of as an interest free loan to the U.S. Treasury. If we multiply the $580 billion in cash by the interest rate of 1% in 2017 on a three month Treasury Bill, then the seigniorage income to the U.S. Treasury from the externally held U.S. currency will be $5.8 billion for 2017.

The U.S. Treasury earns seigniorage income from U.S. currency in the hands of domestic customers within the territory of the United States, as well as U.S. currency held by foreigners abroad. According to the Board of Governors of the Federal System Annual Report of 2010, the cumulative seigniorage earnings, for both domestic and foreign customers, from 1964 to 2010 was in the amount of $916 billion. Of this total amount of $916 billion, the cumulative seigniorage income from 1964 to 2010 coming from U.S. currency held by foreigners amounted to $287 billion.

According to Edgar L. Feige in Crime, Law and Social Change, April 2012, 40% of U.S. cash currency is located in Russia and the former states of the Soviet Union, 27% is held in Latin America, 28% is held in Asia, and the balance of 5% can be found in the Middle East and Africa. According to the Secretary of the Treasury Report of 2006, the top ten foreign countries with holdings of U.S. physical cash currency were reported to be Russia - $80 billion, China - $50 billion, Argentina - $50 billion, South Korea - $15 billion, Turkey - $10 billion, Mexico - $5 billion, Peru - $5 billion, Vietnam - $3 billion, Belarus - $3 billion, and Panama with $2 billion.

Many countries have exchange rate arrangements that depend on the U.S. dollar, such as currency boards using the U.S. dollar, exchange rates that are pegged to the U.S. dollar, and floating exchange rates which are managed and maintained against the U.S. dollar. In 2009, eighty nine countries had pegged their exchange rates to the dollar, which required the monetary policy of these countries to maintain the value of their currencies within rigid bounds relative to the U.S. dollar.

As a store of value, the dollar's status as the most important reserve currency is reflected by the portfolios of foreign governments' foreign exchange reserve accounts. The holdings of foreign exchange reserves of foreign governments skyrocketed from about $1 trillion in 2000 to around $7 trillion in 2010. This huge increase in foreign exchange reserves from 2000 to 2010 was due mainly to developing countries, especially China, which increased its holding of foreign exchange reserves to $2,093 trillion in May of 2009.

According to IMF data, the foreign exchange reserves, excluding gold, for the top 10 countries were as follows: $2,998,200 million for China in January 2017; $1,242,792 million for Japan in October 2016; $751,011 million for Switzerland in April 2017; $492,900 million for Saudi Arabia in April 2017; $435,263 million for Taiwan in October 2016; $400,000 million for Russia in April 2017; $391,500 million for Hong Kong in January 2017; $379,310 million for India in May 2017; $371,100 million for South Korea in December 2016; and $365,295 million for Brazil in December 2016.

According to the IMF Annual Report of 2015, the total reserves of all countries, including gold, was $9,046.9 million at the end of 2014. The advanced economies had total reserves, including gold, of $3,436.9 million at the end of 2014, while the developing economies had total reserves, including gold, of $5,610.1 million at the end of 2014. The share of U.S. dollar assets in the official holdings of foreign exchange, for the advanced economies, at the end of 2004 was 67.2%, and at the end of 2014 was 63.4%. The share of U.S. dollar assets in the official holdings of foreign exchange, for the developing economies, at the end of 2004 was 61.7%, and at the end of 2014 was 62.2%. Thus the dollar share of reserve holdings, in both the advanced and the developing countries, remained at a high level during this ten year period.

As a unit of account, the U.S. dollar plays a crucial role in foreign exchange transactions because world trade is primarily invoiced in the U.S.

dollar. In foreign exchange markets, 84.9% of all foreign currency trading involved the U.S. dollar in 2010.

As a standard of deferred payment, private and sovereign bonds in international markets are extensively denominated in the U.S. dollar. There was a phenomenal growth in the amount of international bonds and notes issued in US dollars between 1994 and 2014. According to data from the website of the Federal Reserve Bank of St. Louis, notes and bonds denominated in U.S. dollars more than quadrupled from $905.89 million in 1994 to $3,782.09 million in 2004, and then more than doubled from $3,782.09 million in 2004 to $8,465.53 million in 2014.

As of July 2016, according to the U.S. Treasury, a total of $6,199.4 billion in Treasury bills, Treasury notes, and Treasury Bonds were purchased by foreigners, which is about half of all Treasury debt issued; the other half of this national debt is owned domestically by Americans. The major foreign holders of Treasury securities are China with $1,185 billion, and Japan with $1,144 billion, as of July 2016. If the U.S. were to default on its debt, it would seriously harm U.S. holders of this debt, as well as foreigners holding this Treasury debt. If the U.S. were to default on its debt, the U.S. dollar would lose its status as the world's reserve currency. In this book I will propose a monetary reform plan that will enable the United States to avoid such a default.

# THE BANKHEAD-PETTENGILL BILL

A few weeks before President Roosevelt was inaugurated as President on March 4, 1933, during the Great Depression, legislation known as the Bankhead-Pettengill Bill was introduced in Congress on February 17, 1933, by Democratic Senator John H. Bankhead of Alabama, and Democratic U.S. House Representative Samuel B. Pettengill of Indiana.

The Bankhead-Pettengill Bill of February 1933 called for the U.S. Treasury Department to issue one trillion dollars of money certificates in the denomination of $1 each. These certificates could circulate as legal tender for the payment of all debts, public and private, and for the payment of all dues, taxes, tariffs, and custom duties, if a two cent postage stamp was affixed to the back of the dollar money certificate each week prior to its changing hands from one user to another. The money certificate would cease to be legal tender if a two cent postage stamp was not affixed on the day of the transfer, and for each week preceding the date of the transfer, as set forth on the schedule on the back of the money certificate. In other words, the money certificate issued under the Bankhead-Pettengill bill would become worthless after every seven days unless a two cent postage stamp was attached to the reverse side of the certificate.

The reverse side of each money certificate would clearly indicate the appropriate place for attaching, each week, a two cent postage stamp, starting from the second Wednesday after the issuance of the certificate, until a total of 52 two cent postage stamps were attached onto the designated spaces during the course of one calendar year. A money certificate that had 52 two cent postage stamps attached on its back could be exchanged at any United States post office for $1 in lawful U.S. currency. According to the text of the Bankhead-Pettengill Bill, "All post offices in the United States are hereby charged with the duty of making such redemption and of forwarding such certificates for cancellation to the Secretary of the Treasury." All money certificates would be destroyed by the United States Treasury, after they were redeemed by the U.S. postal Service for U.S. paper currency, and then forwarded to the U.S. Treasury.

The United States Post Service would pay out $1 for each certificate presented for redemption, but would have collected $1.04 in revenue from the sale of the 52 two cent stamps affixed on the back of each money certificate redeemed at its post offices. If all the money certificates were redeemed by the U.S. Postal Service, the USPS would pay out $1,000,000,000 but would receive $1,040,000,000 from the sale of the postage stamps affixed on the reverse side of the money certificates. This would mean that the USPS would receive forty billion dollars in excess of what it would pay out to redeem money certificates with 52 two cent postage stamps on their backs. In order to carry out its duties under the proposed bill, the USPS would receive forty billion dollars in gross profits from the sale of its stamps affixed on the backs of the certificates. In addition, the USPS would also receive some of the $100 million allotted to the U.S. Treasury to defray the cost of advertising the money certificates by means of posters in post offices and public places, and through advertisements in newspapers and magazines.

Half of the total amount of $1,000,000,000 in money certificates, that is, five hundred billion dollars worth of money certificates would be distributed to the States on the basis of their population in accordance with the fifteenth decennial census, that is, the fifteenth census of the United States conducted in 1930. The amount allotted to each state would be delivered to the governor of the state applying for the quota reserved for his state. The state governments were expected to use the money to spend on infrastructure projects, other construction work, for emergency relief, and for helping the unemployed.

The proposed Bankhead-Pettengill legislation was really a very early form of quantitative easing which would allow the Federal and State governments to directly fund welfare payments, infrastructure projects, and other construction by means of self liquidating money certificates, which would be issued not by the Federal Reserve, but by the U.S. Treasury, an arm of the U.S. government. Unlike the quantitative easing of 2008 in which the Federal Reserve provided trillions of dollars worth of liquidity to banks, the proposed Bankhead-Pettengill bill intended to put cash in the form of money certificates in the hands of tax paying citizens with the right to vote. The issuance of these trillion dollars worth of money certificates would have replaced the spending of at least a trillion dollars worth of taxpayer money on vital infrastructure projects, other much needed construction, and welfare for citizens impoverished by the Great Depression. By using these stamped certificates instead of taxpayer money, the United States Treasury could have saved a trillion dollars worth of the hard earned money of U.S. taxpayers that it had collected in taxes.

Users of the money certificates would be required to pay a usage fee in the form of a two cent postage stamp which they would have to purchase from a U.S. post office in order to affix the two cent postage stamp to the back of the money certificate. The total usage fee of $1.04 in the form of a two cent postage stamp over a fifty two week period would more than fully pay for the $1 face value of a money certificate. This means that the issuer, the United States government, would be more than fully compensated for the cost of redeeming the money certificates, even if the money certificates were initially given away for free. The United States Postal service would realize a gross profit of forty billion dollars after redemption of all money certificates, but because the United States Postal Service happened to be owned by the United States government, in the final analysis, it was the United States government that would have been the ultimate beneficiary of the gross profit of forty billion dollars if the Bankhead-Pettengill bill had been passed by the United States Congress and signed into law by the President.

The Bankhead-Pettengill Bill, introduced in Congress during the final days of the Hoover administration, would have made it possible for the incoming administration of Franklin D. Roosevelt to engage in some desperately needed spending, without incurring additional debt, in order to lift the United States economy that was in such dire straits during the Great Depression. The New Deal programs of President Roosevelt that followed were financed not with money certificates similar to the ones envisaged in the Bankhead-Pettengill Bill, but was instead funded with money borrowed from the Federal Reserve, which only served to exacerbate the U.S. government's problem with debt.

The expansion of credit caused by the injection of one trillion dollars worth of money certificates would have been temporary and self liquidating, and hence would not have led to an erosion in the value of the U.S. dollar in circulation at that time in 1933. In other words, the injection of a trillion dollars worth of the contemplated money certificates in 1933 would not have been inflationary.

The aim of the Bankhead-Pettengill bill was to stimulate the United States economy without the need for the government to obtain money by issuing debt, or by raising taxes. The proposed bill sought to improve economic conditions during the Great Depression by introducing a demurrage charged medium of exchange which would speed up the velocity of transactions. The Bankhead-Pettengill Bill served as a model for Professor Irving Fisher who published the book 'Stamp Scrip' in 1933, and stated, as one of the reasons for writing Stamp Scrip: "There is one other purpose: to unleash a force on which the ultimate cure of the depression really depends."

# THE CONCEPT OF DEMURRAGE

The proposed Bankhead-Pettengill Bill of 1933 which failed to pass in Congress, envisaged the introduction of a trillion dollars worth of money certificates each with a carrying cost of two cents per week. The existence of this fee would have produced a powerful incentive for the holder of the money certificate to get rid of the certificate by spending it before the next date on which the carrying cost of two cents would become due. A medium of exchange, which has this built in feature of a carrying cost associated with it, is referred to as a demurrage charged medium of exchange.

The word demurrage comes from the French word 'demeurer', which means to linger. Demurrage is the penalty that is imposed by a shipping company or a railroad company, on a party that is responsible for the delay in loading or unloading a shipping vessel or a railroad car on time. In other words, the railroad company charges the user a fee called demurrage for each day that the railroad car sits idle on the railway tracks on account of the fault of the party responsible for the use of the railroad car.

When a demurrage fee is applied to a currency, it means that if the currency is not spent within the specified time frame, then a charge similar to a 'parking' fee has to be paid by the user who prefers to hold on to the money. Instead of spending the money so that it is kept in circulation, if a user prefers to hoard the money so that the money is removed from circulation, then a demurrage charged currency will incur a demurrage fee, and the face value of the currency will shrink by the amount of the demurrage fee.

Demurrage is not the same as negative interest. A demurrage charge decreases the face value of a currency, but a negative interest charge does not decrease the face value of the currency. If you borrow $100 worth of an interest free demurrage charged currency with a demurrage rate of 10% per year, and you prefer to hoard this currency rather than spend it, you will have $90 worth of that currency in your possession at the end of one year. If you borrow $100 worth of a currency for one year with no demurrage at -1% negative interest from a bank, the bank will have to give you $1 in interest at the end of the year when it is time for you to return the $100 that the bank gave you as a loan at -1% interest.

If a depositor keeps $100 worth of conventional currency in a bank, as for example the U.S. dollar, and the bank charges the depositor a negative interest of - 1% for holding his/her money for one year, the depositor will have to pay negative interest to the bank. In this case it would be better for the depositor to keep his/her money under the mattress, in the form of physical cash, because paper currency carries an interest rate of 0%. Paper currency is like a negotiable bearer bond, that is, it is a negotiable financial instrument paying zero per cent interest. Anyone in possession of a bank note is anonymously holding a bond issued by the central bank at zero percent interest. The central bank does not know the identity of the holders of its bank notes, and this fact makes it extremely difficult, if not altogether impossible, to assess and collect negative interest charges on paper currency. On the other hand, if a person keeps a demurrage charged currency in a checking account with a demurrage rate of 10% per year, then a demurrage charge of 10/365=0.028% will apply each day. The demurrage fee will be electronically deducted automatically at the specified time each day from the account holding the demurrage money. If the demurrage currency exists only in electronic form, there will be no paper currency in existence to paste postage stamps or some other form of proof of demurrage payment on the back of the paper currency.

The identity of commercial banks who have reserves of base money at a central bank are known because their accounts are registered with the central bank. Consequently the bank accounts of commercial banks at a central bank can easily be electronically debited with negative interest, or for that matter electronically credited with positive interest. Similarly, the bank accounts of people who have money in commercial banks can just as easily be electronically debited with negative interest, or credited with positive interest.

If a currency is not totally electronic, as for example the United States dollar, which exists primarily in electronic form, but also manifests itself as physical cash in the form of Federal Reserve Banknotes, it is possible, but really not practical to apply negative interest rates to such currency. If banks were to apply negative interest rates to U.S. Dollars held in checking or savings accounts, then holders of deposits in checking or savings accounts would pull their money out and hoard their U.S. dollars as cash. This would defeat the purpose of negative interest rates because if interest rates are negative, most depositors would not hold their money in checking or savings accounts. They would prefer to hold their U.S. dollars in cash because of the fact that paper currency carries an interest rate of 0%. It is true that there is a cost of holding, storing, and physically safeguarding physical cash currency, but if the level of the negative interest rate is significant, it will surely be cost effective to pay for the storage of physical cash. For this reason, negative interest rates can work only with currencies that are completely electronic, and have no existence at all as physical cash. According to Cordelius Ilgmann, in his paper entitled Silvio Gesell: 'a strange, unduly neglected' monetary theorist, on page 3:

"Substantial negative rates are today an impossibility because in the current monetary regime there is a limit to the negative rate which can be set, which is given by the zero nominal interest rate on cash (coins and notes) and their storage costs. This floor to rates is called the zero bound to nominal interest rates. It exists because coins and notes are bearer instruments as opposed to registered instruments such as bank accounts (Buiter, 2009, p. 214). Indeed, deducting negative interest from commercial bank reserves or any form of registered account is as trivial as collecting positive interest (Buiter & Panigirtzoglou, 2003, p.730). However, this cannot be done with coins and bank notes, because these are anonymous bearer bonds and their transfer is not registered. Forcing the anonymous holders of notes to pay the interest due is thus impossible, at least with the current form of money. Hence, any attempt to levy negative interest on registered accounts above the carry and storage costs of notes would cause substitution of the former by the latter, given that they are perfect substitutes in the provision of liquidity. Thus, if one wishes to set negative nominal interest rates, it is necessary to submit the whole monetary base to negative interest rates, including of course notes."

The great advantage of electronic money over paper currency lies in the fact that paper currency is primarily suitable for positive interest rates, whereas it is possible for an electronic currency to have any interest rate, positive or negative. Positive interest rates do not provide an incentive for households or businesses to take out loans and spend money during an economic downturn. With a positive rate of interest, a borrower pays back a loan with interest. With an interest free loan, the borrower pays back only the principal amount of the loan. With a loan borrowed at a negative rate of interest, the face value of the loan amount remains unchanged during the duration of the loan, but a borrower pays back less money than the original amount of the loan, because he/she receives an interest payment from the lender when the loan is repaid. This is why negative interest loans or interest free loans can stimulate the economy during a recession or an economic downturn.

Central banks clearly need an ability to set negative interest rates, in their arsenal of available monetary tools, to be able to fight recession and deflation, but unfortunately they do not have the ability to set appropriate negative interest rates given the framework of the current monetary system in which the U.S. dollar and all other major currencies currently exist ot only in electronic form, and also in the form of coins and paper currency. The Swedish Central Bank, the Riksbank, lowered its interest rate to minus 0.25 percent during the financial crisis of 2008, although this was clearly inadequate to stimulate the Swedish economy at that time. In an article in the Financial Times of April 27, 2009, Krishna Guha reported that in order to deal effectively with the financial crisis of 2007/2008:

"The ideal interest rate for the U.S. economy in current conditions would be minus 5 per cent, according to internal analysis prepared for the Federal Reserve's last policy meeting. The analysis was based on a so-called Taylor-rule approach that estimates an appropriate interest rate based on unemployment and inflation. A central bank cannot cut interest rates below zero. However, the staff research suggests the Fed should maintain unconventional policies that provide stimulus roughly equivalent to an interest rate of minus 5 per cent."

A few ways have been suggested in recent years for removing the technological constraint of levying a carry tax on paper currency so that holders of paper money could be forced to pay a holding charge, which would then reduce their desire to hoard money. Marvin Goodfriend wrote in an article entitled, 'Overcoming the Zero Bound on Interest Rate Policy', in the November 2000 issue of the Journal of Credit and Banking:

"To supplement the carry tax on electronic reserves, a carry tax could be imposed on currency by embedding a magnetic strip in each bill. The magnetic strip could visibly record when a bill was last withdrawn from the banking system. A carry tax could be deducted from each bill upon deposit according to how long the bill was in circulation since last withdrawn and how much carry tax was 'past due'. Likewise, a carry tax could be assessed on currency held as vault cash in banks." Professor Gregory Mankiw of Harvard University wrote in an article in the New York Times of April 18, 2009:

"The problem with negative interest rates, however, is quickly apparent: nobody would lend on those terms. Rather than giving your money to a borrower who promises a negative return, it would be better to stick the cash in your mattress. Because holding money promises a return of exactly zero, lenders cannot offer less. Unless, that is, we figure out a way to make holding money less attractive. At one of my recent Harvard seminars, a graduate student proposed a clever scheme to do exactly that. (I will let the student remain anonymous. In case he ever wants to pursue a career as a central banker, having his name associated with this idea probably won't help.) Imagine that the Fed were to announce that, a year from today, it would pick a digit from zero to 9 out of a hat. All currency with a serial number ending in that digit would no longer be legal tender. Suddenly, the expected return to holding currency would become negative 10 percent. That move would free the Fed to cut interest rates below zero. People would be delighted to lend money at negative 3 percent, since losing 3 percent is better than losing 10. Of course, some people might decide that at those rates, they would rather spend the money - for example, by buying a new car. But because expanding aggregate demand is precisely the goal of the interest rate cut, such an incentive isn't a flaw - it's a benefit."

The late Margrit Kennedy who was a professor of architecture at the University of Hannover in Germany, discussed the concept of demurrage money at length in her book that was published in 1987 entitled, 'Interest and Inflation Free Money: Creating an Exchange Medium That Works for Everybody and Protects the Earth'. She wrote on pages 102 & 103 of this book:

"The hoarding of cash in the new system could be avoided much more easily than by gluing a stamp on the back of a banknote as was done in Worgl. Several suggestions have been made: One is a lottery system. It would ensure the circulation of cash by the withdrawal of one specific note denomination, in the same way as a lottery draw. Based on today's eight denominations (in the case of the German Mark DM 5/10/50/100/200/500/1000), e.g., the eight colored balls representing different bank note denominations would be mixed with white balls representing no conversion in such a way that on statistical average - a conversion of one denomination would occur once or twice per year. Draws could take place, for example, on the first Saturday of each month. The drawn notes would remain legal tender and could be used for payment in all shops. However, the respective fee would have to be deducted from payments with these bank notes........Unlike stickers, or stamp money, the drawing of the denominations has the advantage that there is no need to print new money. We could keep the same money we have today and the actual cost of the system would be no higher than the replacement of worn out notes today."

In 2014, Ecuador became the first country in the world to introduce a totally electronic currency based on a law that banned the Bitcoin, and gave the Central Bank of Ecuador a monopoly in issuing electronic currency. Ecuador has not abandoned the U.S. dollar which replaced its own currency, the Sucre, in the wake of an economic and banking crises in the fall of 2010. The new electronic currency, called the Dinero Electronico, coexists in parallel with the U.S. dollar in Ecuador, but unlike the U.S. dollar which circulates as physical cash, the Dinero Electronico is totally electronic. The Dinero Electronico does not have demurrage built into it, and is therefore not a demurrage charged currency. If the Central Bank of Ecuador sets a negative interest rate, it will not cause the Dinero Electronico to behave like a demurrage charged electronic currency. Sweden is fast becoming a totally cashless society just like its Nordic neighbors Finland, Norway, and Denmark. In 2016, only 2% of the value of all payments in Sweden were made in cash, and this is expected to decline further to 0.5% in 2020. When the Swedish Krona becomes totally electronic, will a negative interest rate applied to the Swedish Krona have the same effect as demurrage? The answer is no.

If the Swedish Krona ceases to exist as physical cash in the near future, depositors will not be able to avoid negative interest charges by hoarding their money as cash, and negative interest will cause their money balances in their bank accounts to shrink. In the case of a demurrage based currency, it is possible for users to avoid paying demurrage charges by spending the money before the demurrage charge takes effect. This is the fundamental difference between demurrage and negative interest. An electronic currency that has demurrage built into it can speed up the velocity of circulation of that currency, whereas a totally electronic currency without built in demurrage cannot perform the same function regardless of whether interest rates are positive or negative.

The German monetary and social reformer Silvio Gesell was the first person to propose a currency system based on the concept of demurrage. As the seventh of nine children, Silvio Gesell was born on March 17, 1862 in Sankt Vith, which was then a part of Germany, near the frontier with Luxembourg. Sankt Vith is now in Belgium because the area of Eupen and Malmedy were ceded by Germany to Belgium under the terms of the Versailles Treaty after World War I, and this territory officially became part of Belgium in 1925. Eupen and Malmedy were annexed by Hitler to Germany during World War II, but these areas were returned to Belgium in 1945, and is now a part of Belgium's province of Liege. Most of Belgium's German speaking citizens live in Eupen and Malmedy, although a third of the population of this territory are French speaking Walloons. Gesell's mother was a French speaking Walloon, belonging to the Catholic faith, and his father was a German, belonging to the Protestant faith, originally from the town of Aachen, located about 56 miles from Sankt Vith.

Gesell studied at the local secondary school in Sankt Vith and then enrolled at the grammar school in Malmedy. He had to discontinue his attendance before he could graduate from the grammar school in Malmedy because his parents could not afford to pay for his continued attendance. Gesell then worked for the Deutsche Reichspost, the imperial post office system in Germany, but gave up this civil service position in favor of joining his brother's business in Berlin as an apprentice in 1878. After four years he went to Malaga in Spain to work as a correspondent for two years, until he was compelled to return to Berlin in 1874 to complete his military service. In 1887, he moved to Buenos Aires in Argentina where he started a business for dental equipment, which was a franchise of his brother's business in Argentina. The economic and social crises caused by the depression of 1890 in Argentina severely affected his business, and this made him critically examine the current monetary system. The economic crisis in Argentina made him ponder deeply about the defects in the prevailing currency system, and he struggled to find a solution to the problem.

Silvio Gesell focused his thoughts on the structural defects inherent in the currency and monetary system, and became the first man to develop and expound the concept of demurrage by publishing his ideas on monetary reform in a series of booklets starting in 1891. His first work, entitled Die Reformation im Munzwesen als Brucke zum sozialen Staat (Currency Reform as a Bridge to the Social State) was published in 1891 in Buenos Aires as a short booklet. Again in the same year in Buenos Aires in 1891, he published his fundamental ideas regarding currency reform in another booklet entitled Nervus rerun. This was followed by the publication of many other articles, pamphlets, and booklets, until he retired to his farm at Les Hauts Geneveys in Switzerland in 1906, where he published the first section of his standard work in 1906 entitled, Die Verwirklichung des Rechtes auf dem vollen Arbeitsertrag. Gesell went back to Argentina in 1907, and lived there till 1911, when he returned to Germany to live in the vegetarian commune Obstbausiedlung Eden, located in the north of Berlin. He published the second section of his standard work entitled, Die neue Lehre vom zins, in Berlin in 1911. These two sections of his standard work were combined and published in Berlin and in Switzerland's capital city of Berne, during the first world war in 1916 with the title, Die naturliche Wirtschaftsordnung durch Freiland und Freigeld. The sixth edition of this book was translated into English by Mr. Philip Pye, and was published under the title, The Natural Economic Order.

Silvio Gesell explained in his book that the purpose of money is to facilitate exchange and to eliminate the problems involved in bartering goods and services. In order for money to serve as an efficient instrument of exchange, the properties that money should possess are as follows:

1) Money must be able to secure the exchange of goods and services.
2) Money must be capable of speeding up the exchange of goods and services between buyers and sellers.
3) Money must make the cost of exchange between buyer and seller as little as possible.
4) Money must not be in a form such that it can be taken out of circulation when money is scarce.
5) Money must not be in a form such that the market can be flooded with money when there is already more than enough money in the economy.
6) Money must not be superior as a commodity as compared to the commodities for which it is being exchanged.

The first criterion of good money - that it must be able to secure the exchange of goods and services, can be judged by the absence of trade depressions, high unemployment, or economic or monetary crises. The second criterion of good money - that it must accelerate exchange, can be judged by how rapid the turnover of goods and services is in the economy, and by how much stocks of unsold inventory are increasing in the economy. The third criterion of good money - that it must cheapen exchange, will be judged by the difference in the seller's cost of producing an item and the price paid by a buyer of that item.

The fourth and fifth criteria of good money can be satisfied only by money that is spent or lent into existence as 100% money. In other words, this means that demurrage money can be printed into existence as fiat money by the Federal Reserve, which the U.S. government can then spend, but demurrage money cannot be created by private commercial banks as fractional reserve money. Private commercial banks can only become brokers of preexisting reserves of demurrage money that they have on deposit, or which they have borrowed from the Fed. Private commercial banks will not be able to create demurrage money which, if future monetary reform permits, will coexist in parallel with the traditional U.S. dollar.

However, private commercial banks can continue to create traditional U.S. dollars as bank debt money on the basis of fractional reserve banking.

Finally, the sixth criterion of money - that money as a commodity should not have properties that it make it superior to the commodities for which it is being used as a medium of exchange, can be judged by whether the owners of money are in hurry to spend their money, just like the suppliers of goods and services, who are always in a hurry to sell their goods and services. According to Gesell, on page 119 & 120 of his book, The Natural Economic Order:

"Money is an instrument of exchange and nothing else. Its function is to facilitate the exchange of goods, to eliminate the difficulties of barter. Barter was unsafe, troublesome, expensive, and very often broke down entirely. Money, which is to replace barter, should secure, accelerate and cheapen, the exchange of goods. This is what we demand of money."

Hungry and exhausted after a long and tiresome day's work, three construction workers arrived at a restaurant for dinner. The first worker had a ten dollar bill in his wallet with which he would be easily able to purchase his meal. The second worker only had ten dollars worth of chewing tobacco in his pocket, and he could pay for his meal only if he could find somebody to buy his chewing tobacco. The third worker had no money or goods to exchange, but was willing to work for one hour for ten dollars. The first worker would have no problem in getting dinner, the second worker would find it difficult to get some food at the restaurant, but the third worker would have the greatest difficulty in satisfying his hunger. This story illustrates the superiority of money in our current monetary system over goods and labor. A holder of money can immediately put his money to use at any place or time of his choice, but an owner of goods cannot always so readily trade his goods. To be able to buy right away, a worker cannot always sell his labor immediately at a time and place of his choice. Money enjoys a flexibility of deployment that cannot be matched by goods, services, or labor.

Gesell recognized that the role of money as a medium of exchange was in conflict with its role as a store of value. These two roles of money were clearly in contradiction with each other because, whereas a medium of exchange functions optimally when it circulates, a store of value requires its removal from circulation, or at least a temporary withdrawal from circulation. Unlike goods which are perishable and deteriorate over time, money can be hoarded by its owners without any physical deterioration or cost of storage. Suppliers of goods and services, and providers of labor, are always under pressure to sell their goods or provide their labor as soon as possible, but holders of money can afford to wait as they are under no such compulsion. According to Gesell, on page 122 of his book, The Natural Economic Order:

"As the owners of goods are always in a hurry for exchange, it is only just and fair that the owners of money, which is the medium of exchange, should also be in a hurry."

"Supply is under an immediate, inherent constraint; therefore demand must be placed under the same constraint. Supply is something detached from the will of owners, so demand must become something detached from the will of owners of money."

"If we decide to abolish the privileges enjoyed by the owners of money and to subject demand to the compulsion to which supply is by nature subject, we remove all the anomalies of the traditional form of money and compel demand to appear regularly in the market, independently of political, economic or natural conditions. Above all, the calculations of speculators, the opinions or caprices of capitalists and bankers will no longer influence demand. What we term the 'tone of the Stock-Exchange" will be a thing of the past. As the law of gravity knows no moods, so the law of demand will know of none. Neither the fear of loss nor the expectation of profit will be able to retard or accelerate demand."

Once upon a time, on a certain day, a man who was capable of earning $500 per week was trapped inside a room without food and water because the door to his room was locked from outside. On the same day, the door to a different room full of $1,500 worth of food was locked from outside, and the door to a safe containing $1,500 was locked. After three weeks, when the door to the room where the man was trapped was opened, the man was found dead. On the same day, after three weeks, when the door to the room containing the food was opened, most of the food was found spoilt. After three weeks, when the door to the safe was opened, the $1,500 worth of bank notes were found exactly in the same condition as before. This story goes to show that the characteristics of money as a commodity in our current monetary system are quite different from the characteristics of the commodities that are being exchanged with money as a medium of exchange. According to Gesell, on page 121 of his book, The Natural Economic Order:

"Only money that goes out of date like a newspaper, rots like potatoes, rusts like iron, evaporates like ether, is capable of standing the test as an instrument for the exchange of potatoes, newspapers, iron, and ether. For such money is not preferred to goods either by the purchaser or the seller. We then part with our goods for money only because we need the money as a means of exchange, not because we expect an advantage from possession of the money."

"So we must make money worse as a commodity if we wish to make it better as a medium of exchange."

In an economy which depends on money as the medium of exchange, the supply of goods and services and the demand for such goods and services will be in balance only if the money that is earned by a seller is spent once again. In other words, if a seller hoards the money that has been earned by selling his goods or services because there is no cost in storing money, then there will be a lack of purchasing power for the demand of goods and services of other sellers in the market. According to Gesell, on page 122 of his book, The Natural Economic Order:

"And what do the priceless advantages of compulsory monetary circulation cost us, the producers, who create the money through the division of labour? Nothing but renunciation of the privilege of infecting demand with our arbitrary will, and, through it, with greed, hope, fear, care, anxiety, and panic. We need only abandon the illusion that we can sell our produce without someone else's buying it. We need only pledge ourselves mutually to buy, at once and in all possible circumstances, exactly as much as we have sold. And in order to secure reciprocity for this pledge, we must endow money with properties that will compel the seller of goods to comply with the obligations incidental to the possession of money; we must compel him to convert his money into goods again - personally, if he has any need of goods, or through others, to whom he lends his money, if he has not."

"Are we then willing to break the fetters that enslave us as sellers of our produce, by renouncing our despotic privileges as buyers over the produce of our fellows? If so, let us examine more closely the unprecedented and revolutionary proposal of compulsory demand. Let us examine a form of money subjected to an impersonal compulsion to be offered in exchange for goods."

What exactly is this form of money that Gesell is referring to in the above quotation from page 122 of his book, The Natural Economic Order? Gesell is alluding to his idea of a demurrage charged money which he called Free Money since it would be free of interest. The fact that traditional money can be hoarded puts money holders in the very privileged position of having the power to withhold money from the market and thereby disrupt business and commerce. The power to disrupt economic activity makes it possible for money holders to exact a reward, in the form of interest, in return for loaning out their money instead of hoarding it. If a demurrage fee is built into money, money holders would no longer be able hold money without cost because they would have to pay a periodic demurrage charge for holding on to money. To avoid demurrage fees, money holders would either have to spend their money, or shift their money from demurrage charged checking accounts into savings accounts that neither pay interest, nor charge demurrage. Money in savings accounts would be loaned out by banks without interest to borrowers. According to Gesell, on page 190 of his book, The Natural Economic Order:

"From whatever side we consider the problem of covering the demand for loan-money so completely that interest would disappear; whether we approach the problem from the side of demand or the side of supply, we find that there are no natural obstacles to such covering. Except for the traditional form of money, the road is free for loan money without interest, as well as for houses and means of production without interest. The elimination of interest is the natural result of the natural order of things when undisturbed by artificial interference. Everything in the nature of men as in the nature of economic life urges the continual increase of so called real capital - an increase which continues even after the complete disappearance of interest. The sole disturber of the peace in this natural order we have shown to be the traditional medium of exchange. The unique and characteristic advantages of this medium of exchange permit the arbitrary postponement of demand, without direct loss to its possessor; whereas supply, on account of the physical characteristics of the wares, punishes delay with losses of all kinds. In defence of their economic welfare both the individual and the community have been and are at enmity with interest; and they would long ago have eliminated interest if their power had not been trammelled by money."

When money is hoarded, it interrupts the circulation of the money that is being hoarded. Exchanges of goods and services that could have been possible are prevented from taking place during the time period that this money is hoarded. Let us imagine that a hundred dollar bill which normally changes hands once a month has been hoarded by its owner for one year. The immobilization of this $100 bill will lead to the loss of exchanges worth $1,200 during the one year period that this $100 bill remains inoperative. Money that is withheld from circulation and kept idle leads to a loss in economic activity that is directly proportional to time. Whenever money is hoarded, it loses its function as a medium of exchange, and switches to its other role as a store of value. This possibility of hoarding money constitutes a fatal flaw in our current monetary system because it causes money to switch from a medium of exchange to a store of value during the time interval of the hoarding. Goods can be exchanged with goods in a single step in a barter transaction, but the exchange of goods with money requires two steps: goods for money in the first step, and then money for goods in the second step. The second step will not occur if money is immobilized after the first step. Immobilization of money is like a brake that has been applied to stop additional exchanges of goods and services. According to Gesell, on page 123 of his book, The Natural Economic Order:

"The purpose of Free-Money is to break the unfair privilege enjoyed by money. This unfair privilege is solely due to the fact that the traditional form of money has one immense advantage over all other goods, namely that it is indestructible. The product of our labour cause considerable expense for storage and caretaking, and even this expense can only retard, but not prevent their gradual decay. The possessor of money, by the very nature of the money-material (precious metal or paper) is exempt from such loss. In commerce, therefore, the capitalist (possessor of money) can always afford to wait, whereas the possessors of merchandise are always hurried. So if negotiations about the price break down, the resulting loss invariably falls on the possessor of goods, that is, ultimately, on the worker (in the widest sense). This circumstance is made use of by the capitalist to exert pressure on the possessor of goods (worker), and to force him to sell his product below the true price."

A travelling salesman was passing through the town of Hawarden in Sioux City, Iowa during the height of the Great Depression in 1932. It was a bad time for the inhabitants of this small town who were having a hard time eking out a living. Most of the people were in debt and living on credit. The streets were empty and deserted as the salesman stopped at a motel to check into a room. After paying for his room at the front desk, the salesman gave the clerk a $100 bill to keep in the motel safe, saying that he would pick up the $100 bill the next day at checkout. The clerk, who had an overdue payment of $100 at his dentist's office next door, quickly slipped out surreptitiously and gave the $100 bill to the dentist's receptionist to pay his overdue debt, thinking that he would be able to collect the $100 which his neighbor owed him before coming to work the next morning. The dentist owed $100 to the janitor who cleaned his office, and as soon as he showed up to collect his payment a few minutes after the hotel clerk had left, the dentist's receptionist gave the same $100 bill to the janitor. The janitor was in debt to his local grocer in the amount of $100 for groceries that he got on credit for the past month, so he immediately went to his grocer and retired his debt by handing him the $100 bill. The grocery store owner had a past due bill of $100 from a grocery supplier who happened to walk into his grocery store just as the janitor left. The grocery store owner still had the $100 bill in his hand when he saw his grocery supplier walk into his store, and as soon as he saw him, he immediately gave him the $100 bill to settle his debt. Now the grocery supplier happened to be the motel clerk's neighbor and had borrowed $100 from the motel clerk which was long past due. When the motel clerk had finished his shift at the hotel that day, he went to his neighbor, the grocery supplier, who erased his debt to the clerk by giving him the same $100 bill. The next morning, the motel clerk quickly put the $100 bill in the hotel safe, and as soon as the salesman came for checkout, he took the bill out of the safe and placed it on the counter for the salesman. To the clerk's amazement, the salesman picked up the $100 bill and nonchalantly lit his cigar with it, saying "counterfeit, a fake gift from a crazy friend."

As a result of the use of one counterfeit $100 bill, five people were out of debt in a time period of less than twenty four hours: a motel clerk, a dentist, a janitor, a grocery store owner, and a grocery supplier. This tale of a counterfeit dollar is a graphic description of what can happen in an economy when the velocity of circulation of the medium of exchange is very high. According to Gesell on page 121 of his book, The Natural Economic Order:

"In short, our worthy experts when considering the currency question forgot the goods - for the exchange of which the currency exists. They improved money exclusively from the point of view of the holder, with the result that it became worthless as a medium of exchange. The purpose of money evidently did not concern them, and thus as Proudhon put it, they forged 'a bolt instead of a key for the gates of the market'. The present form of money repels goods, instead of attracting them."

In 1891, in his earliest proposal to establish Free-Money, Gesell suggested in 'Currency Reform as Bridge to the Social State', the use of Tabular Free-Money. In this method, the face value of the Free-Money notes would decrease from 100 at the beginning to 95 at the end of the year. The current value of the note would be shown in a table printed on it.

In the 1916 edition of his book, The Natural Economic Order, Gesell adopted the idea of Stamped Free-Money, suggested by George Nordmann, a Swiss merchant. Instead of losing 5% of their face value during the course of the year, the Free-Money notes would retain their full face year if the holder of the note affixed a stamp each week on the reverse side of the note.

A demurrage fee equivalent to one-thousandth of the face value of the note would be required each week to keep the note valid as legal tender. For a $100 Free-Money note, a ten cent stamp would have to be affixed every Wednesday on the dated spaces provided for this purpose on the back of the $100 Free-Money note by its various holders. For an entire year, fifty two ten stamps worth $5.20, or 5.2% of its face value, would be needed to keep a $100 Free-Money note valid as legal tender.

The currency stamps would be available for purchase in perforated sheets, at a cost of $1 per sheet. A fully stamped Free-Money currency note, with 52 stamps on its reverse, could be exchanged for a new currency note for use in the following year. The number of Free-Money currency notes in circulation would remain the same because one fully stamped Free-Money note would be exchanged for another new Free-Money note. Gesell envisaged the establishment of a Currency Office which would try to stabilize the general level of prices by issuing or withdrawing Free-Money, in accordance with index numbers of prices. According to Gesell, on page 123 of his book, The Natural Economic Order:

'Free-Money is not redeemed by the Currency Office. Money will always be needed and used, so why should it ever be redeemed? The Currency Office is, however, bound to adapt the issue of money to the needs of the market in such a manner that the general level of prices remains stable. The Currency Office will therefore issue more money when the prices of goods tend to fall, and withdraw money when prices tend to rise; for general prices are exclusively determined by the amount of money offered by the existing stock of goods. And the nature of Free-Money ensures that all the money issued by the Currency Office is immediately offered in exchange for goods. The Currency Office will not be dormant like our present monetary administration which with indolent fatalism expects the stability of the national currency from the mysterious so-called 'intrinsic value' of gold, to the great advantage of swindlers, speculators, and usurers; it will intervene decisively to establish a forced general level of prices, thereby protecting honest trade and industry."

# FRACTIONAL RESERVE BANKING

Fractional reserve banking emerged in the middle of the fourteenth century when private Venetian bankers were entrusted with deposits of specie for safekeeping for which they gave deposit receipts to the owners. The owners of the deposits did not always return to reclaim their specie to buy goods or services, but instead found it more convenient to make their purchases with the deposit receipts that they received from the Venetian banks, because the deposit receipts themselves began to circulate as cash for the payment of goods and services. The Venetian bankers soon realized that since all the owners of specie never arrived on the same day to reclaim their specie, they could safely write additional deposit slips and loan them out to borrowers who then used those deposit receipts to buy goods and services in the market. This practice spread to other banks in Venice, Amsterdam, and other cities of Europe, and by the seventeenth century, the goldsmiths of London were making lucrative profits by lending out deposit receipts. When this practice was eventually discovered, it was regarded as a grave breach of trust by the public. However, over the centuries this practice has never been officially outlawed, and today it has evolved into the accepted and lawful practice of fractional reserve banking. Demand deposits have replaced deposit slips and banknotes issued by private banks. Instead of writing deposit receipts or printing private banknotes, as private banks did in the past, banks now make book keeping entries to credit borrowers with demand deposits which they can then spend like real money by writing checks.

All national currencies are at present interest bearing fiat money which is created ex nihilo, (out of nothing), by central banks as central bank reserves (also called base money). Central bank reserves exist as coins and banknotes in the vaults of banks, and as electronic reserves in the computers of central banks. This base money is borrowed from the central bank by private commercial banks and forms the basis on which checkbook money (demand deposits) is then created as bank debt by private commercial banks through fractional reserve banking.

Private commercial banks are not allowed to create central bank reserves; only central banks can create central bank reserves. A private bank must get the coins and currency that it needs from a Federal Reserve bank, which will supply the commercial bank with the requested amount of coin and currency, and then debit the cost of such coin and currency to the commercial bank's account at the Federal Reserve bank. If a commercial bank has a supply of coins and currency that is in excess of what it normally needs, it can send some of the coins and currency back to the Federal Reserve, and its bank account at the Federal Reserve will be credited.

The U.S. Treasury maintains checking accounts with the Federal Reserve in which incoming tax and other revenues are deposited and through which government payments are made. The Federal Reserve issues the nation's coins and paper currency although the U.S. Treasury actually has the coins minted at the Bureau of the Mint, and the paper currency printed at the Bureau of Engraving and Printing. The paper currency and coins are made available to the Federal Reserve at manufacturing cost.

Although depository institutions such as a bank cannot create central bank reserves, they are allowed to practice fractional reserve banking, by means of which they can loan money into existence in an amount that satisfies the legal reserve requirements set by the Federal Reserve. If the legal reserve requirement is 10%, then a bank must maintain reserves of base money in its bank account at the Federal Reserve in the amount of 10% of its outstanding loans. A legal reserve requirement of 10% means that a bank can make loans in an amount equal to ten times the amount of the reserves of base money in its bank account at a Federal Reserve bank. A bank creates checking account money when it loans money to its customers. The promissory note signed by the customer becomes an asset for the bank, while the demand deposit in a checking account for the customer becomes a liability for the bank. This newly created bank credit functions like money and can be used by the customer to make payments.

Customers can write checks on checking accounts to settle debts, make purchases, pay taxes, or obtain U.S. coins or cash. If those receiving these checks deposit them in other banks, these checks will be cleared by the Federal Reserve after deducting the face value of the checks from the reserves of the bank issuing the check. If a bank is short on reserves at the central bank, it can borrow reserves from the central bank or from other banks having accounts at the Federal Reserve. Central bank reserves are the ultimate means of payment between banks. Checks written on bank accounts at different banks are cleared at the central bank by transferring central bank reserves between the accounts of those banks at the central bank.

Normally checks written by customers of different banks tend to offset each other during the check clearing process, and very little base money needs to be borrowed to settle the differences in inflow and outflow of reserves at the end of the day. However, if a particular bank goes on a lending spree, and expands its lending faster than other banks, then it is possible that it may experience a net outflow of its central bank reserves. In other words, its outflow of reserves would be greater than its inflow of reserves. If this bank is unable to borrow reserves from the central bank, or from other banks, it will fail. This is the reason why, in spite of its ability to create money through the practice of fractional reserve banking, a depository institution such as a private commercial bank can fail.

If the legal reserve requirement is 10%, then a bank is supposed to have that much in reserves at the central bank before making a loan to a borrower. If a credit worthy customer walks into a bank and asks for a loan, and the bank wants to make the loan, then a private commercial bank will not be deterred if its reserves at the central bank happen to be insufficient to make the loan. The bank will still make the loan. After making the loan, the bank will swing into action to secure the necessary central bank reserves to meet the legal reserve requirement. The bank will either borrow the reserves from other member banks, or it will get an overdraft from the central bank on its reserve account with the Federal Reserve.

The practice of fractional reserve banking gives private commercial banks and other depository institutions the awesome power of being able to expand or contract the money supply because more than ninety percent of business in the United States is transacted with checkbook money. Whenever banks make loans, money is borrowed into existence, thereby increasing the total volume of demand deposits. When loans are repaid, checking account money is destroyed, thereby decreasing demand deposits by that much. In a normal time period, the expansion and contraction of demand deposits tend to balance each other. When the economy is booming, banks usually make more loans, which drives the boom higher, but in a recession or depression, banks cut back on their lending, thereby intensifying the recession or depression.

The federal funds rate is the rate that the Federal Reserve charges banks for borrowing money. It is also the target rate used for banks lending to each other. After being at zero since 2008, the Fed first raised the federal funds rate to 0.5% in December 2015. It was raised to 0.75% on December 14, 2016. The Federal Open Market Committee raised the federal funds rate to 1% on March 15, 2017. Although a negative interest rate was needed in 2008, the zero bound on interest rates prevented the Federal Reserve from setting a negative interest rate.

# WHY THE UNITED STATES NEEDS A COMPLEMENTARY CURRENCY

National currencies all over the world are debt based, interest bearing fiat currencies manufactured through the mechanism of fractional reserve banking. At present there is a monopoly of this one kind of money that circulates not only nationally, but also internationally. Nationally, this one type of money circulates within the boundaries of a single nation, but internationally the money flows of different nations of this one kind of money interact with each other within the framework of a global monetary system. The dependence of the global monetary system on just this one kind of money is the reason why the world's monetary system is so fragile and prone to systemic crises. According to the IMF, there were 425 economic, monetary, and banking crises in the forty year period from 1970 to 2010.

If a demurrage charged complementary currency is established to coexist in parallel with the traditional conventional dollar, then the United States will have two types of currencies with inherently different properties to fight different aspects of the economic, monetary, and banking crises that it has to contend with from time to time. With two conceptually different currencies operating side by side, the U.S. banking system will be less vulnerable to a banking crisis in the future. The economic and monetary system of the United States will become less fragile and more resilient in the face of a systemic crisis.

A collapse of Bear Stearns in March of 2008 might have resulted in a full fledged financial panic. Fearing this possibility, the Federal Reserve provided a loan to facilitate the takeover of Bear Stearns by JP Morgan Chase. AIG was on the brink of collapse in October of 2008, and the Federal Reserve was convinced that its failure would be the end of the financial system. Fearful of this possibility, the Federal Reserve loaned AIG 85 billion dollars to prevent an AIG collapse. AIG has since repaid this money with interest, but the point is that the government had no choice but to bail out private firms with conventional taxpayer money. In the words of Ben S. Bernanke in his book, The Federal Reserve and the Financial Crisis, on page 86:

"So, the problem we had in September 2008 was we really did not have any tool - legal tools or policy tools - that allowed us to let Bear Stearns or AIG and the other firms go bankrupt in a way that would not cause incredible damage to the rest of the system. And therefore we chose the lesser of two evils and prevented AIG from failing. That being said, we want to be sure that this never happens again. We want to be sure that the system is changed so that if a large systemically critical firm like AIG comes under this kind of pressure in the future, there will be a safe way to let it fail, so that it can fail and the consequences of its mistakes can be borne by its management and shareholders and creditors without bringing down the whole financial system."

There is absolutely no doubt that Dr. Ben S. Benranke is right in his judgement that a change is needed in the system in order to make sure that in the event of a future financial crisis, no financial institution is 'too big to fail'. This is why the United States needs a national complementary demurrage charged electronic currency to coexist with its conventional currency, the United States dollar. In order that the monetary system of the United States may become viable, the United States needs a national complementary demurrage based currency in addition to the conventional U.S. dollar that already exists. If such a complementary demurrage currency is introduced through monetary reform, the Federal Reserve System of the United States will indeed have the necessary monetary tools available to contain any future economic, monetary, or banking crisis which has the potential to bring down the entire global economy.

The conventional money currently in the monetary system is expected to perform several traditional functions such as medium of exchange, store of value, unit of account, standard of value, and standard of deferred payment. It is a fallacy to assume that this one kind of money can effectively play all of these five roles because some of these roles contradict each other. For example, our conventional money cannot function as an efficient medium of exchange and at the same time serve as a convenient store of value. In order to serve as a store of value, this money must be hoarded. Hoarding money will remove it from circulation until its owner decides to spend it or lend it, thereby reducing its velocity of circulation.

The purpose of a demurrage based complementary currency is to speed up the exchange of goods and services in the economy. The built in demurrage fee will encourage holders of this electronic currency to spend it before the demurrage charge is debited electronically at the specified time each day or each week, depending upon how it is set up. This complementary demurrage currency will not play multiple roles which are at cross purposes with each other. Its primary function will be to serve as a medium of exchange, because it is not designed to serve as a store of value. Demurrage is a penalty for not spending demurrage money in an individual's possession, whereas positive interest is the reward for not spending conventional money in an individual's possession. Interest on conventional money cannot be earned by hiding it under a mattress, but it can surely be earned by lending it instead of spending it. Demurrage encourages consumers to engage in consumption, whereas positive interest rewards people if they defer consumption. Conceptually demurrage is different from positive interest, and in practice, where the exchange of goods and services is the lifeblood of a healthy economy, demurrage functions in a way that is the exact opposite of positive interest.

Our conventional money makes investors focus on short term projects rather than long term projects regardless of the merits of a long term project over a short term one. This short term focus on investment projects is caused by the interest bearing nature of money in the current monetary system in which money comes into existence as bank debt, and therefore requires the payment of interest. Interest makes the present value of a long term project less than the present value of a short term project. Present value is the opposite of the more easily understood concept of simple interest. $100 invested today at 5% simple interest will amount to $105 after one year, which means that the present value today of $105 at an interest rate of 5% is only $100. This implies that any investment of $100 in a project that will return $105 after one year will be attractive only if the rate of interest is less than 5%, because it would be better to leave the money in a bank account which pays 5% interest. An excellent example of short term versus long term focus on investments is given by Bernard Lietaer and Jacqui Dunne in their book 'Rethinking Money', on pages 45-46:

"To put it another way, say the same entrepreneur has a choice between two different forestry investments: planting a pine or an oak. With the same interest rate, the short-term thinking process becomes clear when one compares the two. To keep the numbers simple, it is assumed that numbers are inflation adjusted and that the risk of specific investment projects is independent of the time frame. A pine tree can be felled in 10 years and would then bring a yield of $100. An oak, on the other hand, cannot be harvested until it is 100 years old, and it would then be valued at $1,000 per tree. With these assumptions, and if one doesn't have to take interest into account, the two investments could be seen as equivalent, as one could harvest and replant the pines every ten years, ending up with the same $1,000 in 100 years.

"Now the investor asks: What are these two investments worth as seen from today? We saw that with an interest rate of 5 percent, the investment in a pine that will produce a yield of $100 in ten years is equivalent to $61 today. Similarly calculated, with the same interest rate of 5 percent, the value today of the $1,000 oak tree in 100 years is only $7.60! This difference in value of $61 versus $7.60 is due only to the interest feature of the money used. This demonstrates that, while there is a lot of commercial interest in harvesting old growth forest, there is none in planting trees that will take a long time to mature and be harvested.

"More generally, this difference also describes, why, in a society using an interest-bearing currency, financial investments are focusing mainly in the short term."

Unlike conventional money which is interest based, demurrage money is interest free money which will either be spent into the economy or lent to borrowers without interest. The absence of interest makes the complementary demurrage currency favorable for long term investment projects. Unlike interest, a demurrage charge does not cause the future to be discounted, a fact that levels the playing field for long term investment projects to compete favorably with short term investment projects.

For interest based conventional money there is an inverse relationship between the rate of interest and investment - a higher interest rate generates fewer investment projects. This follows from the concept of marginal efficiency of capital which was first introduced by John Maynard Keynes, and is discussed in his book, The General Theory of Employment, Interest, and Money, on pages 135-137. The marginal efficiency of capital is that rate of interest which would equate the price of a fixed capital asset with its present discounted value of expected income. In order to decide about an investment project, a business takes into consideration the marginal efficiency of capital, and the capital requirements of the project. In order for investment to occur in a specific project, the marginal efficiency of capital must be higher than the rate of interest. In simpler words, for investment to occur, the present value of future returns must be greater than the cost of capital.

Suppose an investment project requires an investment of $1,261,186 and is expected to produce a cash flow of $200,000 per year for the next ten years, that is, it will produce a total cash flow of $2 million in the next ten years. If the rate of interest is 10%, then $1,261,186 borrowed at 10% simple interest for 10 years will require a total of $2 million to service this debt. The net present value of this project will be zero because net present value, NPV= The value of future cash flows discounted at the rate of return minus the initial investment. The present value of the expected cash flow of $2 million over ten years at an interest rate of 10% is $1,261,186. The initial investment is $1,261,186, and so the net present value is $1,261,186 - $1,261,186 = 0.

If the rate of interest is 5% instead of 10%, then the cash flow of $2 million over the next ten years has a present value of $1,571,356. Therefore, the net present value of the contemplated investment project at the lower interest rate of 5% will be NPV = $1,571,356 - $1,261,186 = $310,170.

If the rate of interest is zero, the expected cash flow of $2 million over the next ten years has a present value of $2 million. Therefore, if the loan is denominated in interest free demurrage money, the investment project will have an NPV = $2,000,000 - $1,261,186 = $738,814.

As the above example shows, the interest rate has a profound effect on the viability of investment projects and the interest rate determines to a large extent the investment decisions of entrepreneurs in the U.S. economy, or for that matter in the global economy. If a demurrage charged complementary currency operates side by side with conventional currency, investment projects that would not otherwise be viable in our conventional currency, would become possible with loans denominated in the complementary currency.

In the current monetary system, a situation called a liquidity trap emerges when interest rates fall close to zero and yet there are no profitable investment opportunities to be found. An interest rate close to zero means that saving money will yield very little interest for a saver, yet this may not be enough to dissuade people to save. Conventional money cannot persuade people to spend, so that it may be possible to make full use of a nation's productive capacity. If people are collectively unwilling to buy as much as they are able to produce, it means that a portion of the nation's productive capacity is sitting idle. Businesses are unable to put additional people to work despite unused industrial capacity, because overall demand for their products remain too low. The Federal Reserve can saturate the economy with liquidity, but it cannot force people to spend their conventional dollars to lift the economy out of the liquidity trap. During a recession or in a severe economic downturn, the Federal Reserve needs to set negative interest rates which are impossible because of the zero bound on physical cash currency.

Conventional paper currency can be dropped from helicopters and collected by people as they fall on the ground, but there is no guarantee that this money will be spent by people who come into possession of this money. Rather than spend this money, people in possession of this money may choose to save it for a rainy day. Unless this drop of money from the sky is spent, there will be no change in income, and consequently no change in the nation's output of goods and services. Electronic demurrage money cannot be dropped from the sky, but it can surely be credited electronically to an individual's checking account. An individual receiving this kind of money will be more inclined to spend it on goods and services before it starts diminishing in his or her account.

Given a 100% electronic complementary demurrage currency, the Federal Reserve will have some powerful monetary tools at its command to address the problems associated with a liquidity trap. A negative interest rate is not needed on demurrage currency that will be held in checking accounts because checking account money is subject to demurrage. Demurrage money held in a checking account will be subject to demurrage but demurrage money in savings accounts neither receive interest, nor are they subject to demurrage charges. If demurrage money is moved from a savings account to a checking account, then the demurrage charges that would have accumulated upto that point in time will be applied. With a complementary demurrage currency, it is not only possible to provide zero interest loans to borrowers, but it is also possible to provide loans with a built in incentive of principal reduction, such that with every on time payment, the borrower will get a reduction of, say 1% of the remaining principal balance. Borrowers who make monthly payments on time will be rewarded with a reduction of the remaining amount that they owe on the loan.

Private commercial banks will lend preexisting reserves of demurrage money but will not be able to create it like conventional money by the fractional reserve method. The Federal Reserve will print reserves of 100% fiat demurrage currency which will exist only in electronic form in its computers, and it will make these reserves available to the U.S. Treasury in exchange for zero interest Treasury bonds which the U.S. Treasury department will issue for this purpose. The U.S. Treasury Department will make these reserves of electronic demurrage currency available to private commercial banks and other financial institutions for lending to individuals and businesses. Banks and other financial institutions will act as brokers but not creators of demurrage currency, and will be paid a fee at the time of making the loan for originating and servicing the loan.

Does it make sense financially for the U.S. Treasury to provide interest free demurrage money to borrowers through private commercial banks? After a borrower has borrowed demurrage money, say for example to purchase a house from a builder, the proceeds of the loan will be placed in the builder's checking account where it will immediately incur demurrage. The builder will pay his subcontractors and others and demurrage charges will be imposed on their checking accounts. The act of placing the loan proceeds in a checking account will immediately start generating demurrage revenue for the U.S. Treasury. During the life of the loan, the

U.S. Treasury will not only collect the monthly payments on the loan, but it will also collect the stream of demurrage payments from the principal amount of the loan which will be circulating in demurrage checking accounts. This is the deep dark secret of how an interest free demurrage loan can make money for its lender!

Not convinced that an interest free demurrage loan can generate more revenue than a loan with interest in traditional U.S. dollars?

For a 30 year loan in the amount of $100,000 at 5% simple interest, the required payment would be $536.82 per month, and the total payments collected over the life of the loan would be $193,256.52. This loan would generate $93,256.52 more than the original amount of the $100,000 loan.

For a 30 year loan in the amount of 100,000 in demurrage money at zero percent interest, the required payment would be 277.78 per month, and the total amount collected from the borrower over the life of the loan would be 100,000. The borrower's monthly payment would be cut almost in half. A payment of only 277.78 would be required in a complementary demurrage currency as compared to $536.82 that is necessary every month to service a conventional dollar loan at 5% interest.

With such outrageously low monthly payments, the borrower is not likely to default on his or her interest free loan, and so the odds are very high that the U.S. Treasury will be repaid with the entire amount of the 100,000 loan. In addition, the U.S. Treasury will not only receive 10% per year in demurrage, which amounts to 300,000 over the life of the loan, but actually the U.S. government will keep receiving demurrage fees in the amount of 10,000 every year for an indefinite period of time!

An interest free loan denominated in demurrage currency has the potential to generate far greater revenue than a conventional loan at interest in U.S. dollars. Both from the borrower's and the lender's perspective, an interest free demurrage loan is far superior to a conventional loan at interest in U.S. dollars. The borrower gets drastically lower monthly payments, while the lender, the U.S. treasury, keeps earning this wonderful tax on money, called demurrage, for an indefinite period of time!

Demurrage fees will be levied on money at a specified time every day in every checking account that has demurrage money. This carrying cost of money can be shifted from one person to another, but can never be eliminated. Someone will have to pay this carrying cost of money as long as it exists in someone's checking account. To avoid paying demurrage, an individual can place it in a savings account, where it pays no demurrage and receives no interest; but demurrage money in a savings account cannot be spent unless it is again shifted to a checking account, at which time the accumulated demurrage fees will be imposed. The fact that demurrage money can be held, but not spent in a savings account, means that demurrage money will be held primarily in checking accounts so that people can defray their expenses with it.

# THE SMART U.S. DOLLAR

Let us give a name to the new national complementary demurrage currency for the United States. Let us call this new currency that will coexist in parallel with the traditional U.S. dollar as the SMART dollar, which we will abbreviate as $SM. This new complementary currency will be a completely electronic independent United States currency which will be freely traded in national and international currency exchanges. This new currency known as the Smart dollar will be created as a fiat, demurrage charged currency by the Federal Reserve. The U.S. Treasury receives U.S. dollars in exchange for Treasury securities which the Federal Reserve buys in the open market from banks and dealers. The U.S. Treasury will receive Smart dollars in exchange for Treasury securities which pay no interest. To differentiate these interest free Treasury securities from other interest bearing Treasury securities, we will refer to these new interest free Treasury securities as sovereign bonds. Legislation that establishes the Smart dollar will clearly state that demurrage fees collected from the use of Smart dollars belong to the United States government, and as such will be remitted directly to the U.S. Treasury.

Smart dollars will be spent into the U.S. economy by the U.S. Treasury or it will be lent into the economy by the Federal Reserve or the U.S. Treasury through private commercial banks and other financial institutions. Demand for this new currency will be very strong from borrowers who are likely to prefer this new currency instead of the conventional U.S. dollar because of its interest free nature. Loans denominated in Smart dollars will have to be repaid in Smart dollars, which will create an enormous demand for this new currency. In all probability, the demand for the new demurrage currency will far outstrip the supply of this new currency. We can safely predict that our new complementary currency will be worth more than our traditional U.S. dollar in the currency exchange markets, and will be a stronger currency in terms of its purchasing power in domestic and international markets.

The United States is in dire need of a second currency that is stronger than the current U.S. dollar because the U.S. dollar's role as the world's reserve currency poses a dilemma for the country's economy. Polish economist Feliks Mtynarski in his 1929 book, Gold and Central Banks, was the first to point out that under a gold standard, as the volume of a particular reserve currency held by foreign investors increases, the reserves of gold held by the country issuing that reserve country comes under pressure. Foreigners holding the reserve currency would begin to doubt if they would be able to convert that reserve currency into gold, if that particular reserve currency was issued indiscriminately.

In the context of the Bretton Woods agreement of 1944, the Belgium born American economist Robert Triffin explained in 1961 that in order to supply the world with reserve currency, it is necessary for the United States to run current account deficits, thus becoming more and more indebted to foreigners, and making the United States unsustainably burdened with debt. The U.S. dollar's reserve currency status causes a negative balance of payments because the inflow of dollars is not enough to balance the outflow of dollars necessitated by the need to supply foreigners with U.S. dollars. The United States is confronted with a conflict between its national and global monetary policies because it is using its one and only currency to serve as the global reserve currency. If the United States wishes to retain the U.S. dollar as the world's reserve currency, then it has no choice but to establish a second parallel complementary currency for the needs of its domestic economy.

The U.S. government has always shown an unwavering commitment to pay the interest on its debt obligations, and Congress has never changed this commitment. The U.S. Treasury has always faithfully paid the interest on its outstanding Treasury obligations which have specified rates of interest and must be paid as scheduled in order to avoid default. A debt default would damage the full faith and credit of the United States government.

The excellent credit rating of the United States government, both at home and abroad, would be ruined. U.S. Treasury bills, notes, and bonds are considered the safest and most dependable securities for foreign investors in international financial markets. This reputation of U.S. Treasury securities would be in tatters in the event of a default. Treasury securities would lose their position as the world's number one in financial securities.

The time is fast approaching when U.S. debt will no longer be considered a dependable and safe asset to hold as a store of value, because it is becoming doubtful if the U.S. will be able to service this debt. When this point in time is reached, U.S. debt will not be considered risk free, and there may be a foreign sell off of U.S. securities that could drive up U.S. interest rates, and make it far more expensive to service the debt. The worst case scenario is the possibility of a U.S. default on its debt, which will trigger an economic collapse worse than the Great Depression.

The debt ceiling for the United States is determined by legislation. Once the United States is at or very close to the debt ceiling, as specified in prior legislation, it is not possible for the U.S. treasury to issue new Treasury securities, or to pay the interest on securities that are about to mature. The total amount of Treasury securities is more than the grand total of all bank deposits in the U.S. banking system. If the debt ceiling prevents the U.S. Treasury from paying interest on Treasury securities as they become due, then the entire financial system will be in a crisis.

Commercial banks hold large amounts of Treasury securities, and if these Treasury securities are ever in default because of non payment of interest, then commercial banks would be unable to complete transactions which involve the use of these securities. The whole financial system would be in chaos. The current monetary system requires that the debt ceiling be raised whenever the United States is at or near the debt ceiling in order to avoid a financial collapse.

Sovereign Treasury bonds being non interest bearing, will not require any interest payment when they mature, and so the debt ceiling has no effect at all on the issuance and performance of these sovereign bonds. The U.S. Treasury will be able to continue making payments in Smart dollars in the event that the U.S. Congress is deadlocked on the issue of the debt ceiling, thus temporarily halting payments in traditional U.S. dollars. If the U.S. Treasury runs out of conventional U.S. dollars to pay its bills during a debt ceiling deadlock, the United States government can still continue to operate by paying its bills in Smart dollars until Congress is able to reach an agreement on raising the debt ceiling. There is no question of the U.S. Treasury being in default of non payment of interest on sovereign bonds, because sovereign bonds will not be interest bearing debt instruments.

The grave problem of budget and trade deficits require imaginative thinking and an unconventional approach to a conventional problem. We cannot tackle the problems caused by our massive and bourgeoning debt with the use of outdated and ineffective monetary tools that we currently have in our possession. We need a modern and conceptually different kind of money to address our massive debt problem. We cannot take the wholesale risk of totally replacing our current monetary system with an untried, untested, and unknown monetary system. But we can, and must make incremental changes to our current monetary system. The introduction of the Smart dollar is an innovation that is urgently needed to modernize the current monetary system of the United States.

# THE NATIONAL DEBT

The national debt provided the wherewithal for the United States to fight for freedom until the British acknowledged the United States as a sovereign and independent nation by signing the Treaty of Paris on September 3, 1783. Indeed, it is fair to say that the United States was born in debt. The national debt enabled the fledgling nation to successfully prosecute the war of 1812 with Great Britain and thus retain its independence as a sovereign country. During the war of 1912, Washington DC was captured on August 24, 1814, and the marauding British forces torched the White House and the U.S. Capitol before withdrawing from the U.S. capital 24 hours later. The war of 1812 was ended by the Treaty of Ghent that was signed by Britain and the U.S. on December 24, 1814. The United States could neither have come into existence, nor survived as an independent nation without the help of the national debt.

During the 1860s, the Union was saved by the national debt which financed $2,182 billion of the total accumulated deficit of $2,614 during the Civil War, while the printing of greenbacks financed $432 billion of the total accumulated deficit of $2,614 billion. In the first World War, it was the national debt that brought victory for the U.S. and its allies. The accumulated national debt jumped from $2,975,619,000 in 1917 to $25,484,506,000 in 1919 - an increase of about $22.5 billion in just two years. Again, in the 1940s, it was the national debt that saved the world from Hitler. The national debt soared from $72,422,445,000 in 1942 to $269,422,099,000 in 1946 - an increase of approximately $197 billion.

The accumulated national debt skyrocketed from $269,422,099,000 in

1946, to the mind boggling amount of $19,844,544,000,000 on June 30, 2017 - an increase of $19,575,121,901,000. The national debt has multiplied 73.65 times during the last 71 years. The period from the U.S. declaration of independence on July 4, 1776, to the formal Japanese surrender on September 2, 1945, was marked by major wars, panics, depressions, and banking crises. The national debt proved to be an invaluable asset during this period, helping to finance wars and making it possible to alleviate the fluctuations in the business cycle.

But from 1946 to 2017, the United States has been embroiled in smaller wars which pose no existential threat, yet these smaller wars have consumed trillions of dollars that eventually raised the level of national debt. The national debt came to the rescue when the United States was on the verge of a systemic collapse in 2008, but the national debt may not be able to repeat this performance in the event of another future economic meltdown.

The national debt has been a blessing in disguise for the United States for the most part of its history, but after serving the United States faithfully for over two hundred years, the national debt, which is now almost twenty trillion dollars, may have become the Achilles Heel of the United States economy.

According to the U.S. Bureau of economic analysis, federal debt as a percentage of real GDP has increased from 45.1% in 2000 to 119.9% in 2016. The interest payment necessary to service the federal debt is the amount of debt multiplied by the rate of interest. Increasing levels of debt to GDP and increasing rates of interest result in an increasing percent of the nation's GDP that will be necessary to service the debt. In other words, increasing levels of debt can only be paid for by a commensurate increase in the nation's GDP. Unfortunately, U.S. GDP growth will not be enough to service future debt. According to the Bureau of Labor Statistics, the projected annual growth rate for the period 2014 to 2024 is only 2.2%. In the absence of adequate GDP growth, how will the United States avoid a default on its debt?

Raising additional revenue through tax increases, cutting entitlements, broadening the tax base, and raising effective tax rates are methods which might have worked decades ago, but these methods really cannot solve the problem of the national debt at the present time. Theoretically, it is possible for the government to levy additional taxes to generate the funds necessary to pay off the national debt in a matter of years, and the taxation method would have worked when the proportion of the national debt owned by foreigners was not very high. Paying off the debt when foreigners held very little of our national debt would have resulted in a redistribution of income in the domestic economy. Income would have been transferred from those paying the taxes to those receiving repayment of the debt, but the total income of the U.S. economy would have remained almost the same, because decades ago foreigners held very little of the national debt.

Foreigners held only 4% of the national debt during the 1960s, and 15% in 1986. Despite low interest rates, foreigners held 32% of the total public debt outstanding in Treasury securities as of December, 2016. It is not a realistic option at present, to raise U.S. dollars through taxation to pay off foreign creditors, because doing so may reduce the total income of the U.S. economy. As the enormous debt to foreign investors is paid off, trillions of dollars will flow out of the United States unless it is recycled back through the purchase of U.S. goods and services, or through foreign investment in the United States.

There is also the problem of redistribution of income if taxation is used to pay off the entire national debt held by U.S. citizens and foreigners. The national debt is held by foreign investors, the Federal Reserve, mutual funds, state and local governments, private pension funds, banks, insurance companies, and people in higher income brackets. In the current monetary system, heavy taxes would reduce the aggregate spending of those in lower and middle income brackets. It is unlikely that this reduction in aggregate expenditure of low and middle income people would be offset by an increase in the aggregate spending of higher income people who would be the recipients of debt repayments. It is unlikely because the marginal propensity to consume of higher income people who will receive the debt repayment money, would be less than the marginal propensity to consume of lower and middle income people who would pay the taxes to enable the government to pay off the national debt. Aggregate demand would also decline if foreigners who have been repaid do not recycle the money back into the United States by investing in the U.S. or by purchasing U.S. goods and services. Thus, total spending in the economy will be reduced, and the economy will contract, in the event of repayment of the national debt in the current monetary system. Any attempt to pay off the national debt in an economy under the fractional reserve system may bring about an economic downturn, or serve as a catalyst for a recession or depression.

Is the national debt a burden that will be passed on to future generations? If we look at the effect of the repayment of the national debt on the economy as a whole, it is clear that while some people will pay taxes, other people will be recipients of tax repayments. For the economy as a whole, it is impossible to pass the real cost of the national debt to future generations. However, the problem of redistribution of income from people in low income levels who pay the tax to pay off the debt, to higher income people who receive the tax repayments, may cause spending to decline because the marginal propensity to consume of higher income people is less than the marginal propensity to consume of lower and middle income people. Without reforming the current monetary system, it would very risky for the government to embark on a program to pay off the national debt by raising taxes, because it may result in a mild economic slump at best, or a severe economic recession at worst.

While it is true that the real cost of the national debt cannot be passed on to future generations for the economy as a whole, it is also true that the individual burden of the national debt can be passed on to future generations. If the government decides to pay off the national debt in the same generation that the debt was incurred, then people in that particular generation would have to give up their purchasing power in an amount necessary to pay the taxes required to pay off the debt. If the government postpones the repayment of its debt to the next generation, then the descendants of people of the original generation will suffer a loss of purchasing power to an extent necessary to pay the taxes required to pay off the debt. The undeniable fact is that while people in the generation that the national debt was incurred have enjoyed the benefits of the national debt, their descendants in the next generation will have to shoulder the burden of paying taxes, should the government decide to pay off the national debt through taxation in the next generation.

Billions of dollars of the national debt become due and payable annually, and at times when the U.S. Treasury does not have the money to service maturing debt, the Treasury issues new Treasury bonds, bills, and notes to raise the funds necessary to pay off maturing debt. In practice, it is not always that easy to sell enough new Treasury securities within a short period, and so the government is compelled to pay higher rates of interest which, of course, raises the cost of issuing new debt to replace maturing debt.

There have been several attempts by Congress to reduce debt, the first of which was the Balanced Budget and Emergency Deficit Control Act of 1985 that President Reagan signed into law on December 12, 1985. Also referred to as the Gramm-Rudman-Hollings Act, it required Congress to reduce the budget deficit each year so that the budget would be in balance by 1991. To balance the budget by 1991 required huge spending cuts. To avoid these massive spending cuts, the Reagan administration postponed the balanced budget requirement to 1993 by amending the Gramm-Rudman-Hollings Act in 1987. In spite of these legislative efforts, the budget deficit in 1991 was $220 billion, just one billion less than the deficit of $221 billion in 1986.

In response to the failure of the government to reduce deficits, Congress passed the Budget Reduction Act of 1990 which called for deficit reduction in the amount of $500 billion over five years beginning in 1991. Nonetheless, budget deficits continued to increase, climbing to $269 billion in 1991, and $290 billion in 1992. Again, Congress responded by passing the Revenue Reconciliation Act of 1993 which aimed to reduce the federal deficit over a five year period through spending cuts and increased taxation. This was followed by the Balanced Budget Act of 1997 which called for a balanced budget through spending cuts and increased taxation.

From 1993 to 1998, there was a decline in federal deficits, and the first federal surplus of $69 billion occurred in fiscal 1998. This was followed by a federal surplus of $124 billion in 1999, a federal surplus of $236 billion in 2000, and another federal surplus of $128 billion in 2001. Soaring tax revenues in conjunction with cutbacks in discretionary federal spending resulted in federal surpluses in four consecutive years that began in 1998, and ended in 2001. The federal surpluses which totaled $557 billion from 1998 to 2001 was the basis for a prediction by the Congressional Budget Office that the total of federal budget surpluses would reach $3 trillion by the year 2011. The Balanced Budget Act of 1997 was allowed to expire.

The federal surpluses recorded from 1998 to 2001 proved to be short lived because deficits returned in 2002, and have occurred every year since then. As of June 30, 2017, the total public debt outstanding in U.S. Treasury securities has soared to $19,844,544,000,000. Under the current monetary system, repeated legislation by Congress has failed to reduce or eliminate our national debt.

# PAYING OFF THE NATIONAL DEBT

In the dual currency system that I am proposing in this book for the United States, the U.S. Treasury, in coordination with the Federal Reserve, will set the rate of demurrage for the complementary currency. If the rate of demurrage is set at 10% per year, then the U.S. Treasury will receive 10% of the total amount of demurrage currency in circulation each year. If there is one trillion of Smart dollars in circulation in a particular year in the U.S. economy, the U.S. government can expect an income of one hundred billion Smart dollars in demurrage fees in that particular year. With ten trillion of the new complementary demurrage currency in circulation in checking accounts in the U.S. economy, the U.S. Treasury can expect to collect one trillion worth of demurrage, which is essentially a tax on holding money, on this new currency called Smart dollars every year.

The U.S. Treasury can exchange its income of one trillion in smart dollars for traditional U.S. dollars in the currency exchange markets. If it does so, it should get at least $1 trillion in U.S. dollars with which it can pay down its national debt which happens to be denominated in U.S. dollars, or pay other obligations denominated in U.S. dollars. There is a big difference between a country's debt that is denominated in its own currency, and a country's debt that is denominated in a foreign currency. To pay off the debt owed to foreigners in a foreign currency, a country first has to acquire that currency by exchanging its own currency in foreign currency markets, which puts downward pressure on its currency's value. In simpler words, the value of a country's currency will fall in world currency markets if it tries to exchange a large amount of its currency for another foreign currency.

In the case of the United States, foreigners are holding a vast amount of debt that is denominated in the country's own currency. During the fiscal year 2016, the United States paid a total of $432.65 billion in interest payments on its debt. In April 2017, foreign creditors owned $3.9 trillion in U.S. debt, of which Japan held $1.1 trillion, and China held $1.09 trillion. This debt can be paid off completely in a matter of a few years with demurrage income from Smart dollars, thereby eliminating more than a hundred billion dollars in interest payments to foreign holders of U.S. debt each year. As the United States gradually pays down its debt, future increases in the debt to GDP ratio will be arrested, and the debt to GDP ratio will then gradually decline until it reaches a more sustainable level.

China has been slowly selling its holdings of U.S. debt because in November of 2013 it held $1.3 trillion versus $1.09 trillion in April of 2017. Whenever China sells Treasury bills, notes, or bonds, the Chinese Yuan appreciates against the U.S. dollar. What this means is that the U.S. dollar's value depends upon the willingness of its foreign creditors to hold U.S. debt, because whenever foreigners sell U.S. debt, the U.S. dollar declines in value against their currencies. By accumulating U.S. debt, foreigners are able to prevent their currencies from appreciating against the U.S. dollar, and consequently they are able to sell their products at a lower price in the U.S. market, to the detriment of domestic manufacturers. The power to prevent their currencies from appreciating against the U.S. dollar by not selling their U.S. debt gives these countries a big advantage in international trade. If foreigners conclude that it is not in their interest to hold U.S. debt, and decide to dump their U.S. debt, then the value of the U.S. dollar will drop precipitously. However, if the United States pays off its debt to foreigners gradually, the exchange rate of the U.S. dollar in currency markets will adjust itself gradually, and its products will once again become competitive in world markets.

If the U.S. pays off the $3.9 trillion debt owed to foreigners, then foreign creditors will be deprived of the power to dump their U.S. debt, simply because they will no longer have a huge amount of U.S. debt in their hands. By paying off the debt owed to foreigners, the U.S. Treasury will save hundreds of billions in interest paid to foreigners each year, and at the same time stave off the possibility of a debt default. The uncertainty regarding the future of the U.S. dollar as the world's reserve currency will be removed once and for all. The U.S. will then have the Smart dollar as a strong currency, and a conventional dollar as the world's reserve currency, whose exchange rate will allow U.S. goods and services to be competitive in world markets.

What are foreign creditors going to do with the trillions of dollars in their hands when the U.S. pays back their debt? Since the U.S. dollar is the world's premier reserve currency, the first option is that they can easily exchange their dollars into any other currency of their choice. If this option is exercised to exchange dollars for Indian rupees, then the foreign investor will have Indian rupees in an Indian bank, while the Indian bank will have an equivalent amount of U.S. dollars in a correspondent U.S. bank. The second option is to buy assets anywhere in the world from sellers that accept payment in U.S. dollars, in which case the seller will have to deposit the U.S. dollars in a U.S. bank, or a local non U.S. bank that has a banking relationship with a correspondent U.S. bank. The third option is to purchase goods and services from the United States, in which case the dollars received in payment will be deposited in a U.S. bank. The exercise of any of these three options will result in U.S. dollars still remaining in U.S. banks because U.S. dollars cannot leave the U.S. financial system. If an English investor deposits U.S. dollars in a British bank, the U.S. dollars will be held on behalf of the British bank in a correspondent U.S. bank, with which the British bank has a banking relationship.

Once the Smart dollar becomes a reality, there will be a fourth option for the foreign creditors who have received trillions of U.S. dollars in exchange for their U.S. Treasury securities denominated in U.S. dollars. This option for them will be to exchange their conventional U.S. dollars for demurrage charged Smart dollars, and then purchase sovereign U.S. Treasury bonds denominated in Smart dollars. Sovereign U.S. Treasury bonds will neither pay interest, nor incur demurrage fees, but they will be backed by the full faith and credit of the U.S. government, and will be as safe and dependable as conventional U.S. Treasury securities. Holding deposits of large amounts of money in the form of sovereign bonds will be far less risky than keeping large amounts of U.S. dollars in traditional banks or other financial institutions. Sovereign bonds will not have any maturity date since they do not pay interest, and will be 'cashed' by depositing the sovereign bond in a Smart dollar checking account at any time. Of course, as soon as the sovereign bond is deposited in a Smart dollar checking account, demurrage fees will be debited at the specified time each day.

The gradual elimination of U.S. Treasury securities denominated in U.S. dollars, will slowly but surely relieve the United States from the burden of interest payments on its Treasury debt obligations. Treasury securities have existed since 1790, when the total amount of treasury debt stood at $71,060,508.50. As of June 30, 2017, the total public debt outstanding in Treasury securities was $19,844,554,000,000 which is approximately twenty trillion dollars. There has been a relentless increase in the total amount of outstanding Treasury debt over the years from $71 million in 1790 to $19.84 trillion in 2017. Treasury debt has never been paid off but the interest on the debt has always been paid. The burden of interest payments has existed since 1790. The United States paid a total of $432.65 billion in interest on Treasury debt during the fiscal year 2016. When Treasury debt denominated in U.S. dollars is replaced with debt issued as sovereign bonds denominated in Smart dollars, the U.S. will not have to pay interest on this kind of debt. Sovereign bonds can permanently ease the burden of interest on the national debt because there will be no interest payable on sovereign bonds. When this happens, the term 'national debt' will become a misnomer because debt implies payment of interest. It will be possible to hold sovereign bonds indefinitely without any cost. Interest bearing national debt will cease to exist.

Sovereign bonds will not incur demurrage fees, and hence will be useful and popular as a financial instrument to park money safely without any carrying cost. Sovereign bonds will be a vehicle for individuals and businesses to park their Smart dollars safely without risk. Interest bearing Treasury debt can be gradually phased out and replaced with sovereign bonds. The issuance of sovereign bonds will not change the amount of money in the economy. The purchase of a sovereign bond will result in a transfer of Smart dollars from the purchaser to the U.S. Treasury. Smart dollars will change hands, but there will be no change in the amount of Smart dollars in the economy, which will remain the same.

The fact that there will be no change in the total amount of Smart dollars when sovereign bonds are bought or sold implies that the quantity of sovereign bonds traded will not affect the smart money supply of the economy. Large quantities of sovereign bonds can be issued without shrinking the supply of Smart dollars in the economy because whenever sovereign bonds are sold, the proceeds of the sale of sovereign bonds will go directly to the U.S. Treasury, which can then pump the Smart dollars back into circulation in the economy by using smart money to pay its bills, or by lending the smart money through commercial private banks or other financial institutions. For this reason, there will always be enough sovereign bonds available to supply the needs of foreign countries who need to park the U.S. dollar reserves that they have accumulated by running trade surpluses with the United States or other countries. Rather than take the risk of keeping large quantities of U.S. dollars in private commercial banks, or for that matter in nationalized commercial banks, foreign countries will prefer to convert their U.S. dollars into Smart dollars, and then park them in safe, liquid, and secure sovereign bonds without any holding cost, or maturity date.

The role of the U.S. dollar as the world's premier reserve currency will be buttressed by the existence of a second national complementary currency. The United States will not have to go into debt in order to finance trade deficits which are a corollary of the U.S. dollar's role as a reserve currency. Friction between the United States and its trading partners will be at a minimum because there will no longer be any reason to level charges of currency manipulation at countries accumulating large stashes of U.S. dollars.

Foreign investors can invest in U.S. corporate equities or engage in direct foreign investment in the United States. These are two other choices that they have, but both of these options involve taking risks that foreign investors might find unacceptable, unlike safe and dependable sovereign bonds. As opposed to conventional interest bearing securities which are issued over different time periods at different rates of interest to suit the liquidity preferences of buyers, a sovereign bond will have no maturity date. It will be a highly liquid financial instrument in that it will be possible to convert this financial instrument into cash at any time simply by placing the sovereign bond in a smart money checking account.

The highly liquid sovereign bond will have great appeal to foreign investors to whom the liquidity of the financial instrument is more important than the reward of an interest payment. In simpler words, some investors will prefer to hold a bond that can be converted into cash without loss at any time, instead of a bond that has a maturity date.

# THE MONEY SUPPLY IN A DUAL CURRENCY MONETARY SYSTEM

The money supply in an economy with one conventional currency with fractional reserve banking is equal to the monetary base multiplied by the money multiplier. The monetary base is the sum of the electronic reserves held by banks at the Federal Reserve plus all cash currency in circulation. The money multiplier is the inverse of the fractional reserve requirement. If the reserve requirement is 10%, then the money multiplier is 1/10% = 10. The money supply of the United States in the current monetary system with a reserve requirement of 10% is ten times the amount of its monetary base.

Changes in the money supply is the result of open market operations during which the Federal Reserve buys or sells securities. Legally, the U.S. Treasury can sell a limited amount of Treasury securities directly to the Federal Reserve. The legal limit of the amount of government bonds that the U.S. Treasury can sell directly to the Federal Reserve can be easily evaded if the Treasury department first sells Treasury securities to the public or to banks, and the Federal Reserve then buys those securities from the public or from banks. The intermediaries involved will collect a commission for their services, but other than that there is no difference between a direct sale of bonds by the Treasury to the Federal Reserve, or an indirect sale of government bonds to the Federal Reserve via the public or via banks. Most of the time, the Federal Reserve buys or sells government bonds from private commercial banks or from securities dealers usually in an auction during open market operations. If a securities dealer sells $1 million worth of Treasury bills to the Federal Reserve in an auction, it will receive a check for $1 million in base money (central bank reserves) drawn on a Federal Reserve bank. When the securities dealer deposits this check in his own bank account, his bank balance will increase by $1 million. As soon as the bank presents this check to a Federal Reserve bank, it will be credited with $1 million in central bank reserves in the bank's reserve account at the Federal Reserve bank. The money supply and central bank reserves will both rise immediately and simultaneously by $1 million. When the Federal Reserve sells Treasury securities, the reverse will happen, that is, a reduction in the nation's money supply will occur.

Reserve requirements, which the Federal Reserve has the power to change, is an instrument of monetary policy, just like purchases and sales of government bonds, and the setting of the central bank's interest rate called the federal funds rate. A lower reserve requirement means that commercial banks can expand the money supply on the basis of its existing reserves because the money multiplier, which is the inverse of the reserve requirement, will increase. A higher reserve requirement will decrease the money multiplier, leading to a decrease in the money supply. Reserve requirements represent a step along the road at the ultimate end of which lies 100% reserve banking.

The proposed electronic demurrage charged complementary currency, the Smart dollar, will be based on 100% reserves, and cannot be created by private commercial banks through fractional reserve banking. Only the Federal Reserve System will have the power to create Smart dollars by buying sovereign Treasury bonds, either directly from the U.S. Treasury, or from banks and securities dealers. Unlike self liquidating money certificates which were proposed in the Bankhead-Pettengill bill in 1933, Smart dollars will exist permanently after they are spent into the economy by the U.S. Treasury, or lent into existence through private commercial banks or other financial institutions. Conventional money that is borrowed into existence is destroyed when it is repaid, but Smart dollars will not be destroyed when they are repaid, because Smart dollars will not be loaned into existence. Smart dollars will be manufactured by the Federal reserve before they are loaned. The lending or the repayment of Smart dollars will not affect the supply of Smart dollars in the economy. As a product of 100%

reserve banking, the supply of Smart dollars in the economy will not be influenced by changes in reserve requirements. Demurrage charges applied to Smart dollars will reduce the face value of the complementary currency in checking accounts, but all demurrage charges will be instantaneously remitted to the United States Treasury, and so there will be no change in the overall supply of Smart dollars.

Economist Irving Fisher proved that the total economic output, or GDP as it is now called, depends on the quantity of money in circulation, and the velocity of money in circulation. Also known as the equation of exchange, it means that total spending in a given time period is equal to the amount of money multiplied by the velocity of circulation of money. If an economy has one $1 banknote, and this $1 banknote changes hands 100 times in a month, then the total spending for the month would be $100. This is expressed as:

MV = Total Spending = Total Economic Output = GDP

Where M is the quantity of money in circulation, and V is the velocity of circulation, which is the number of times that this money circulates in a given time period. The quantity of money or the money stock is an amount of money at a certain point in time, and is a stock concept. Money income is the amount of money earned in a unit of time, such as $1,000 per month, or $12,000 per year, and is therefore a flow concept. According to Professor Irving Fisher in his book, The Purchasing Power of Money:

"In each sale and purchase, the money and goods exchanged are ipso facto equivalent; for instance, the money paid for sugar is equivalent to the sugar bought. And in the grand total of all exchanges for a year, the total money paid is equal in value to the total value of the goods bought. The equation thus has a money side (the left side of the equation) and a goods side (the right side of the equation). The money side is the total money paid, and may be considered as the product of the quantity of money multiplied by its rapidity of circulation. The goods side is made up of the products of quantities of goods exchanged multiplied by their respective prices."

With two national currencies coexisting side by side, the total money supply in the United States will be the sum of the amount of conventional U.S. dollars in circulation and the amount of the complementary Smart dollars in circulation. The conventional dollar will be used both for savings and exchange, but the complementary currency, the Smart dollar, will serve only as a medium of exchange. The velocity of circulation of each currency in the economy will be quite different. In an environment where there are two currencies in operation, Fisher's equation must be modified as: M1 V1 + M2 V2 = Total Economic Output = Gross Domestic Product, where M1 is the quantity of money of the U.S. dollar, V1 is the velocity of circulation of the U.S. dollar, M2 is the quantity of money of the Smart dollar, and V2 is the velocity of circulation of the Smart dollar.

Logically, a currency that is being used only as a medium of exchange, and not as a store of value, will have a higher velocity of circulation than the currency that is playing the dual role of a medium of exchange and a store of value. Mathematically this can be expressed as V2 > V1, since the velocity of the Smart dollar will be much higher than the conventional dollar. The higher velocity of the Smart dollar will tend to increase the total economic output, that is, the Gross Domestic Product of the United States.

In the single currency dollar system, changes in the money supply can be effected by changing reserve requirements, but there is no mechanism to directly increase the velocity of the conventional dollar. According to the Quantity Theory of Money, the total money supply in a single currency economy is related to the GDP by the following equation:

MV = P1Q1 + P2Q2 + P3Q3 + P4Q4 + ......PnQn = GDP

The left side of the above equation is the total money paid, which may be considered as the product of the quantity of money M, multiplied by the velocity of money V. The right side of the equation is made up of the products of quantities of goods Q1, Q2, Q3, Q4 ......Qn exchanged multiplied by their respective prices P1, P2, P3, P4 ......Pn. The letter n denotes the number of transactions in the economy.

According to the above equation, the nominal GDP of an economy will increase, but the real GDP may not increase if the quantity of money is increased while the velocity of circulation of money remains the same. This is because the total spending or GDP depends upon the four variables M, P, Q, and V. The number of transactions n, will not increase unless V, the velocity of circulation increases. Therefore, when velocity is constant, either the quantities of goods exchanged, or the respective prices of the goods exchanged will have to increase for GDP to increase. If the increase in the money supply causes prices to rise, then price inflation will be the result. Real GDP is calculated by adjusting the nominal GDP for price inflation. Real GDP will always be less than nominal GDP when there is price inflation. Thus, if an increase in the money supply causes prices to rise, there will be an increase in the nominal GDP of the economy, but not necessarily an increase in real GDP.

In the conventional dollar system, it is not possible to directly change the velocity of money V. The velocity of money changes as a result of changes to the money supply and the GDP:

$V = GDP/M$

The gross domestic product of an economy is the total amount of spending, which is the same as the total money income, or the total economic output of the economy in a specific time period. The supply of money in the economy is also referred to as the money stock. The increase in money income can only exceed the increase in money stock if the velocity of circulation increases during the given time period. Thus, the ratio GDP/M can increase only if V increases.

If the velocity remains constant, increasing the money supply tends to increase the GDP, and/or increase the price level. If the velocity of money remains the same, reducing the money supply tends to reduce the GDP, and/or decrease the price level. According to the late economist Milton Friedman, "inflation is always and everywhere a monetary phenomenon" in a single currency conventional dollar economy.

In their magisterial work, A Monetary History of the United States, published in 1963, Milton Friedman and Anna Jacobson Schwartz showed that from 1867 to 1960, the money stock of the United States multiplied 157 fold in the course of 93 years. The money stock in 1867 was $1,590 million, and in 1960 it was $278 billion, which is an annual rate of 5.4% in the nation's stock of money over the 93 year period. According to the website of the Federal Reserve Bank of Minneapolis, $1 in 1850 had the same buying power of $29.37 in 2017. As the money supply of the United States economy has expanded over the years, the conventional U.S. dollar has lost its value due to inflation. The loss of purchasing power of the conventional dollar as a consequence of price inflation proves conclusively that by its very nature our traditional dollar is not an inflation free currency.

We need a complementary currency that will not lead to price inflation

*Hussain Zahid Imam*

if the money supply is increased. The built in demurrage charge will produce a higher velocity of circulation in the Smart dollar, and so an increase in the money supply of Smart dollars will lead to a higher GDP without price inflation at best, or very little price inflation at worst.

# THE PROBLEM WITH DEFICITS

According to the National Income and Product Accounts (NIPA) published by the Bureau of Economic Analysis (BEA) of the U.S. Commerce Department, the total economic output, that is the Gross Domestic Product, GPD, is determined by the following equation:

GDP = C + I + G + NEX   where

C   is consumer spending
G   is government spending
I    is investment spending

NEX is the difference between exports and imports of products, services, investment incomes and unilateral transfers

If a product or service is consumed or used up immediately, or over a relatively short period of time, then it is classified as personal consumption or consumer spending. If a product or service is used up over a specific period of time, that is, if it is depreciated over a certain period of time, then it is classified as investment spending. Products and services that are exported are not consumed within the United States, but the production of these goods and services is a part of the total output, that is, the GDP.

The current account balance, CAB, is determined by the following equation:

CAB = Total Output - Total Spending

Total Output = GDP = C + I + G + NEX and Total Spending = C + I + G   therefore,

CAB = C + I + G + NEX - (C + I + G)   or

CAB = NEX = difference between exports and imports of products, services, investment incomes, and unilateral transfers.

Although the current account includes investment income and unilateral transfers such as remittances from workers, the current account consists predominantly of the balance of trade, that is, the difference between exports and imports. If we leave out investment income and unilateral transfers from the above equation, the current account balance, CAB, is simply:

CAB = Exports - Imports

When exports are equal to imports, the current account balance is zero. When exports are greater than imports, the current account balance is positive. When imports are greater than exports, the current account balance is negative.

A positive current account balance reflects a current account surplus, and leads to an export of products and services in an amount larger than the import of products and services. In order to balance a current account surplus, there must be a net outflow of capital to finance the purchase of investment assets outside the United States.

A negative current account balance reflects a current account deficit which means that there has been an import of goods and services in an amount that is more than the amount of goods and services that has been exported. A negative current account balance means that there is a trade deficit. In order to balance a current account deficit, there must be a net inflow of capital into the capital account. In other words, if imports are not paid for by exports, then they must be paid for by the sales of real assets such as land, building, etc., or financial assets such as stocks, corporate bonds, treasury bills, notes, bonds, et cetera.

A budget deficit occurs when a government's expenditures are in excess of its revenues. The U.S. federal budget deficit for the fiscal year 2016, which covers the period from October 1, 2015 to September 30, 2016, was $587 billion. The federal budget deficit of $587 billion in fiscal year 2016 was $149 billion more than the federal budget deficit of $438 billion for the fiscal year 2015. In fiscal year 2016, the federal budget deficit was higher than in previous years.

The accumulation of budget deficits plus other borrowing over the years results in what is called the national debt. The national debt at the end of the fiscal year 2016, that is on September 30, 2016, was in the amount of $19,573,444,713,936.79, which is approximately 19.573 trillions of dollars. The debt held by the public was $14.173 trillion, and intra governmental holdings was $5.400 trillion. This does not include state and local debt, and it does not include the so called "agency debt".

Agency debt is the amount of debt outstanding issued by federal agencies such as FHLB and GNMA, and government sponsored enterprises such as Fannie Mae and Freddie Mac. As of now (August 2017), agency debt has not been included in the total debt of the United States Government as published by the United States Treasury. The composition of the federal debt held by different sectors was as follows in December, 2016:

Foreign investors - $6.281 trillion
Federal Reserve - $2.463 trillion
Mutual Funds - $1.379 trillion
State & Local Governments (including their pension funds) - $874 billion
Private Pension Funds - $544 billion
Banks - $570 billion
Insurance Companies - $304 billion
U.S. Savings Bonds - $169 billion
Other - $1.349 trillion
(Individuals, government sponsored enterprises, brokers & dealers, bank personal trusts and estates, corporate & non corporate businesses, and other investors.)

The national debt is issued in Treasury bills with a maturity date of one year or less, Treasury notes with maturities ranging from two to ten years, Treasury bonds with maturities longer than ten years, Treasury inflation protected securities, and special State and Local Government series securities.

The debt held by social security and all other retirement and pension funds amount to nearly half of all U.S. Treasury debt; the other half is held by foreign investors. If the United States were to default on its debt, it would seriously harm current and future retirees, as well as foreign investors. Therefore, a default by the United States on its outstanding debt obligations is unthinkable. A default on U.S. Treasury debt would precipitate a severe financial crisis.

The budget deficit for a particular year is the difference between federal outlays and Federal receipts for that particular year, but the budget deficit for a specific year is not always what the federal government borrows in that year. Other borrowing is equal to the increase in federal debt minus the federal budget deficit. In other words, the increase in federal debt in a specific year is the result of adding the federal budget deficit to other borrowing in that specific year.

There was a federal budget surplus in the years 2000 and 2001, but in each subsequent year from 2002 to 2016, there was a federal budget deficit ranging from a low of $158 billion in 2002 to a high of $1.413 trillion in 2009. From fiscal year 2001 to fiscal year 2016, the federal debt more than quadrupled from $3.394 trillion to $14.434 trillion - an enormous increase of $10.946 trillion over a period of fifteen years.

The interest payment in 2001 on the federal debt of $3.394 trillion held by the public was $210 billion, but because of much lower interest rates, the interest payment on the federal debt of $10.946 trillion held by the public in 2016 was $233 billion. According to the Congressional Budget Office, the projected interest payments on the federal debt held by the public are projected to increase from $270 billion in 2017 to $714 billion in 2026, an increase of $444 billion over the next decade - a projected increase in interest payments of 164.5%. Where will the money to pay this enormous amount of $714 billion of interest in 2026 come from? In a cover story in the April 14, 2016 issue of Time magazine, James Grant writes:

"The public debt will fall due someday. (Some of it falls due just about every day.) It will have to be repaid or refinanced. If repaid, where would the money come from? It would come from you, naturally. The debt is ultimately a deferred tax. You can calculate your pro rata obligation on your smartphone. Just visit the Treasury website, which posts the debt to the penny, then the Census Bureau's website, which reports the up-to-the-minute size of the population. Divide the latter by the former and you have the scary truth: $42,998.12 for every man, woman, and child, as I write this. In the short term, the debt would no doubt be refinanced, but at which interest rate? At 4.8%, the rate prevailing as recently as 2007, the government would pay more in interest expense - $654 billion - than it does for national defense. At a blended rate of 6.7%, the average prevailing in the 1990s, the net federal interest bill would reach $913 billion, which very nearly equals this year's projected outlay on Social Security."

To prevent or reduce budget deficits, the U.S. government must either cut its spending, or generate additional revenue by raising taxes, or allow the dollar to depreciate so that the debt is worth less to debt holders, or reduce the trade deficit. Cutting spending or raising taxes are not realistic options given the high debt to GDP ratio which is approaching 100%. It will not be easy to depreciate the dollar because it is the world's reserve currency, but even if it is somehow possible to devalue the dollar, interest rates on Treasury securities would have to go up in order to prevent investors from fleeing the Treasury bond market. It is possible to reduce the trade deficits that lead to budget deficits, but to accomplish this we would first need to reform the current monetary system of the United States. The monetary reform that is needed is the focus of this book.

The U.S. has never defaulted on its debt, but a U.S. government default on its debt would have terrifying consequences. The U.S. would be unable to pay the salaries of federal employees or military personnel. Social Security, Medicare, and Medicaid payments would cease, as would payments for student loans, tax refunds, and payments needed to keep government facilities open. The U.S. government would not be able to pay the interest on its Treasury debt obligations, in which case the U.S. Treasury debt market would collapse, and the U.S. would lose its ability to borrow. The U.S. dollar would lose its status as the world's reserve currency.

# MONETARY TOOLS IN THE DUAL CURRENCY ECONOMY

Electronic currencies, which coexist with the U.S. dollar as the official currency, have been introduced by Ecuador and El Salvador, but these currencies are not demurrage based. A demurrage based national complementary currency has not yet been introduced by any country, and consequently there are no current studies on the velocity of circulation of such a currency operating in a dual currency system. Between 1932 and 1934, a demurrage charged local currency was established in the Austrian town of Worgl. The experiment with this demurrage currency was quite successful, until the intervention of the Austrian central bank stopped the use of this currency. It has been documented that the velocity of circulation of this demurrage charged money was between twelve to fourteen times faster than the official Austrian currency.

The Federal Reserve will be able to effect changes in the money supply of Smart dollars by buying and selling sovereign bonds directly from and to the U.S. Treasury. However, reserve requirements and interest rates cannot be used as monetary tools in the new complementary currency because Smart dollars will be based on 100% reserves. As an interest free currency, interest rates will not be possible with Smart dollars. The rate of demurrage will be a powerful monetary tool that can be used to speed up transactions. The Federal Reserve Board in Washington DC and the U.S. Treasury will jointly set the rate of demurrage.

The lower bound on interest rates prevents interest rates from being set below zero in the conventional monetary system because the U.S. dollar exists in the form of physical cash. The problem with the zero bound in the current monetary system is explained by Professor Atif Mian and Professor Amir Sufi on page 53 of their book, House of Debt:

"The zero bound means that interest rates cannot get low enough to actually induce savers in the economy to start buying. If interest rates cannot decrease enough, the gap in spending left by levered households cutting back remains unfilled. This is also referred to as the 'liquidity trap,' because when an interest rate is kept at zero when it needs to be negative, people save their money in liquid instruments such as cash and U.S. government treasury bills. Instead of spending, savers hoard money in risk-free assets."

Despite the fact that a positive or negative rate of interest cannot be applied to the Smart dollar, the problem associated with the zero bound in the conventional system can be finessed by providing loans in Smart dollars with a built in incentive of principal reduction, such that with every on time payment, the borrower would get a reduction of, say 1% of the remaining balance. This means that with every on time payment, the borrower's principal balance would be reduced by 1%. This outcome is similar to what would happen in a conventional dollar loan taken out at a negative rate of interest.

Sellers of goods and services are almost always inflationists because they prefer higher prices and want to get as much money as possible for their goods and services in order to maximize their profits. Buyers of goods and services, on the other hand, are generally deflationists, because a buyer wants the prices of the goods that he is purchasing to be as low as possible. That is how a buyer can afford to buy more things for a given sum of money. In this respect, a demurrage charged currency favors the seller, because it forces the buyer to make a purchase in order to avoid paying demurrage fees on the Smart dollars in his checking account.

Deflation occurs when prices fall because the supply of goods is greater than the demand for those goods. Lack of consumer spending in the single conventional currency monetary system is the main culprit responsible for deflation. Lack of spending translates into a lack of demand for goods that have already been produced, and businesses can only get people to buy those goods by reducing the prices of those goods. Lower prices for goods and services may be good for consumers, but lower prices will reduce the profitability of the firms producing those goods, and business firms will respond by cutting back production, and laying off workers in an effort to stay in business.

Laid off workers have to decrease their spending, which then results in lesser demand for goods and services, and more deflation. A spiral of falling prices and increasing deflation comes into play, and it is difficult to combat this deflationary spiral with conventional money. Traditional U.S. dollars cannot prevent a lack of spending. Deflation caused by a lack of spending is impossible with a demurrage charged currency because the demurrage fee makes people and businesses spend their demurrage money, and so there is no lack of demand for goods and services.

If companies are able to lower prices by cutting the cost of production through the use of improved technology, or by lowering their interest costs when they borrow money, then such deflation does not hurt the economy. But deflation caused by a lack of spending can ripple through the economy, causing unemployment, business failures, and bankruptcies. In a deflationary period, the real value of debt goes up when prices are falling. Each dollar of debt unpaid becomes a bigger dollar. Debtors can reduce the number of dollars they owe by repaying their debt, but the value of each remaining dollar owed will go up faster than they can repay. According to the late Professor Irving Fisher, "The more the debtors pay, the more they owe."

A demurrage charged currency works against deflation, and so the rate of demurrage can be used as a monetary tool by the Federal Reserve to fight the threat of deflation. With an interest bearing currency, sellers of goods and services have to pay interest to finance their purchases of equipment, inventory, and sometimes even payroll, and this interest expense is included in the prices of all goods and services. Sellers will not have to pay interest on loans denominated in Smart dollars, hence they can charge lower prices in Smart dollars for their goods and services. By enabling sellers to charge lower prices, a demurrage currency will help to counter inflation.

The national debt cannot be repaid without affecting the money supply under the current system of a single currency. When a business or an individual sells Treasury securities directly to the U.S. Treasury, the money supply does not change because the transaction is completed with preexisting money which the government has obtained through taxation. When the Federal Reserve System sells government securities, the money supply in the economy is reduced. According to the workbook, Modern Money Mechanics, published by the Federal Reserve Bank of Chicago, on page 11, originally written by Dorothy M. Nichols in May 1961, and revised by Anne Marie Gonczy in June 1992:

"Suppose the Federal Reserve System sells $10,000 of Treasury bills to a U.S. government securities dealer and receives in payment an 'electronic' check drawn on Bank A. As this payment is made, Bank A's reserve account at a Federal Reserve Bank is reduced by $10,000. As a result, the Federal Reserve System's holdings of securities and the reserve accounts of banks are both reduced $10,000. The $10,000 reduction in Bank A's deposit liabilities constitutes a decline in the money stock."

In the same workbook, on page 11, Modern Money Mechanics, originally written by Dorothy M. Nichols in May 1961, and revised by Anne Marie L. Gonczy in June 1992:

"Just as purchases of government securities by the Federal Reserve System can provide the basis for deposit expansion by adding to bank reserves, sales of securities by the Federal Reserve System reduce the money stock by absorbing bank reserves."

# THE DEBT TO GDP RATIO

According to the U.S. Bureau of Economic Analysis, federal debt as a percentage of real gross domestic product has increased relentlessly from 45.1 percent in the year 2000 to 119.9 percent in 2016. This level of debt is unsustainable, and any further increase in this level of debt will cause GDP growth to slow down, as has been demonstrated by other important economies of the world, such as Japan, which has a very high debt to GDP ratio.

Douglas W. Elmendorf, a Harvard Professor, who served as the Director of the bipartisan Congressional Budget Office from 2009 to 2015, said in his testimony before a Senate committee in July 2009:

"Under current law, the federal budget is on an unsustainable path - meaning that federal debt will continue to grow much faster than the economy over the long run. Although great uncertainty surrounds long-term fiscal projections, rising costs for health care and the aging of the U.S. population will cause federal spending to increase rapidly under any plausible scenario for current law. Unless revenues increase just as rapidly, the rise in spending will produce growing budget deficits and accumulating debt. Keeping deficits and debt from reaching levels that would cause substantial harm to the economy would require increasing revenues significantly as a percentage of gross domestic product (GDP), decreasing projected spending sharply, or some combination of the two."

Dr. Elmendorf's above testimony in the year 2009 appears to have been very prescient, in that seven years later, federal debt as a percentage of the gross domestic product, was at 119%. In other words, the federal debt is now greater than the nation's GDP. The national debt has to be serviced either from the nation's total income (GDP), or by issuing more debt as maturing debt is retired. It is predicted that the absolute amount of federal debt will grow faster than the absolute amount of GDP in the coming decade, meaning that the debt to GDP ratio will be higher by the end of the next decade unless steps are taken to remedy the situation.

The impact of ageing on public debt was examined in a Bank of International Settlements paper of March 2010 entitled, The Future of Public Debt: Prospects and Implications, written by Stephen G. Cecchetti, Madhusudan S. Mohanty, and Fabrizio Zampolli. The BIS paper makes a set of 30 year projections for the path of the debt/GDP ratio in the 12 industrial economies of Austria, France, Germany, Greece, Holland, Ireland, Italy, Japan, Portugal, Spain, the United Kingdom, and the United States. The authors made four assumptions in their study: 1) Total government revenue will remain at a constant percentage of GDP at the 2011 level. 2) Non age related spending will remain at a constant percentage of GDP at the 2011 level. 3) The real interest rate that determines the cost of funding during the 30 year projection period will remain constant at its 1998-2007 average. 4) The potential real GDP growth rate will be set according to the OECD estimated post-crisis rate. With these assumptions, in the baseline scenario, debt/GDP ratios are predicted to rise rapidly in the coming decade (2010-2020), surpassing 300% of GDP in Japan, 200% in the United Kingdom, and 150% in Belgium, France, Ireland, Greece, Italy, and the United States. The fraction absorbed by interest payments would rise from 5% to 10% in all countries. The BIS study provides the following conclusion:

"Our examination of the future of public debt leads us to several important conclusions. First, fiscal problems confronting industrial economies are bigger than suggested by official debt figures that show the implications of the financial crisis and recession for fiscal balances. As frightening as it is to consider public debt increasing to more than 100% of GDP, an even greater danger arises from a rapidly ageing population. The related unfunded liabilities are large and growing, and should be a central part of today's long-term fiscal planning. It is essential that governments not be lulled into complacency by the ease with which they have financed their deficits thus far. In the aftermath of the financial crisis, the path of future output is likely to be permanently below where we thought it would be just several years ago. As a result, government revenues will be lower and expenditures higher, making consolidation even more difficult. But, unless action is taken to place fiscal policy on a sustainable footing, these costs could easily rise sharply and suddenly. Second, large public debts have significant financial and real consequences. The recent sharp rise in risk premiums on long-term bonds issued by several industrial countries suggests that markets no longer consider sovereign debt low-risk. The limited evidence we have suggests default risk premiums move up with debt levels and down with the revenue share of GDP as well as the availability of private saving. Countries with a relatively weak fiscal system and a high degree of dependence on foreign investors to finance their deficits generally face larger spreads on their debts. This market differentiation is a positive feature of the financial system, but it could force governments with weak fiscal systems to return to fiscal rectitude sooner than they might like or hope. Third, we note the risk that persistently high levels of public debt will drive down capital accumulation, productivity growth and long-term potential growth."

According to the CIA's world factbook of 2017, the debt/GDP ratio in 2016 of the above countries were as follows in 2016: Austria - 85.8%; Belgium - 106.7%; France - 96.5%; Greece - 181.6; Holland - 63.7; Ireland - 77.9%; Italy - 132.5%; Japan - 234.7%; Portugal - 126.2%; Spain - 99.6%; United Kingdom - 92.2; United States - 73.8%.

The BIS study, The Future of Public Debt: Prospects and Implications, seems to have more or less correctly predicted the trend in the debt/GDP ratio of the 12 industrial countries named in the study. It is possible that the BIS study may vindicate itself as the correct prognosticator of the future of public debt.

The Federal reserve held $2.463 trillion worth of Treasury securities as of December 2016. The Federal Reserve would have to sell its entire inventory of $2.463 trillion worth of government bonds for the national debt to be repaid in its entirety. Such a massive sell off of government bonds will surely lead to a significant contraction in the money supply of a single currency monetary system. In a dual currency system, the conventional currency, the smart dollar, will be exchanged in currency markets in order to repay the national debt. This will finesse the problem of any change in the money supply because any reduction to the existing quantity of U.S. dollars caused by the sell off of government securities will be offset by an equivalent supply of U.S. dollars obtained by the U.S. Treasury by exchanging Smart dollars in currency markets.

Once the national debt denominated in traditional U.S. dollars is gone, sovereign Treasury bonds will replace interest bearing Treasury bonds, notes, and bills. Sovereign bonds will be interest free financial instruments without any maturity date, and without any holding cost. The non interest bearing nature of a sovereign bond means that such a bond will only be a financial instrument for parking Smart dollars, unlike a debt instrument which requires interest payments. The issuance of sovereign bonds will not result in an unsustainable debt burden for the United States. The possibility of a United States debt default would be removed forever. The threat of an economic or monetary crisis posed by the possibility of a debt default would also be removed. Te United States will be able to handle future deficits without going into interest bearing debt. The debt to GDP ratio of the United States will gradually improve as the national debt denominated in U.S. dollars is gradually repaid in a matter of years.

# PUBLICLY ISSUED MONEY VERSUS PRIVATELY ISSUED MONEY

The current monetary system in the United States manufactures two kinds of money. The first type of money is publicly issued money that is created by the Federal Reserve debt free at the moment of creation, and this money is known as base money, central bank reserves, or high powered money. This debt free fiat money is created ex nihilo, that is, it is created out of nothing, and exists as electronic reserves in the computers of the Federal Reserve System. The Federal Reserve can lend this money to the U.S. Treasury in exchange for government bonds, but there is a legal limit as to how much government bonds the Federal Reserve can buy directly from the U.S. Treasury. The U.S. Treasury can circumvent this legal limit by selling government bonds directly to commercial banks and the public, which are then sold to the Federal Reserve. The Federal Reserve can also lend base money to private commercial banks which have bank accounts at the Federal Reserve, but base money cannot be borrowed from the Federal reserve by members of the public, businesses, or banks that are not members of the Federal Reserve System. Base money also includes coins and Federal Reserve banknotes which the U.S. Treasury provides to the Federal Reserve at manufacturing cost. The coins are minted at the U.S. Mint, and the banknotes are printed at United States Bureau of Engraving and Printing, both owned by the United States Treasury. Base money is really publicly issued money despite the fact that Federal Reserve banks are privately owned. The Federal Reserve is an arm of the United States government, as the late Professor Milton Friedman explained in his book, Money Mischief, on page 206:

"There is much confusion about whether the Federal Reserve System is a branch of the government or a private enterprise. That confusion has sparked a host of 'crank' conspiracy literature.

The Board of Governors of the Federal Reserve System is composed of seven members, all appointed by the president with the aid and advice of the Senate. It clearly is a branch of the government.

The confusion arises because the twelve Federal Reserve banks are federally chartered corporations, each with stockholders, directors, and a president. The stockholders of each bank are the member banks of its district, and they select six of its nine directors. The remaining three directors are appointed by the Board of Governors. Each member bank is required to purchase an amount of stock equal to 3 percent of its capital and surplus. So, nominally, the Federal Reserve banks are privately owned.

However, dividends paid on the stock are limited to 6 %. Any income in excess of costs is turned over to the U.S. Treasury ($97 billion in 2015). The Board of directors of each district bank names the managing officials of the bank. However, the Board of Governors has a veto power and in practice has often played the major role in naming the presidents of the district banks.

Finally, the most important policy body in the system, other than the Board of Governors itself, is the Open Market Committee, which has as members the seven governors plus the twelve bank presidents. However, only five of the presidents have a vote at anytime, so that the Board of Governors is guaranteed ultimate control.

In short, the system is in practice a branch of the government, despite the smokescreen of nominally private ownership of the district banks."

The second type of money is privately issued money created by private commercial banks as bank debt through the practice of fractional reserve banking. Money that is borrowed into existence as debt is also fiat money that is created out of nothing by private banks. When a bank makes a loan, it creates a demand deposit, which is also known as a transaction deposit, or a checkable deposit. The demand deposit is a liability for the bank, but this liability is balanced by the promissory note of the borrower, which is an asset for the bank.

Privately issued bank debt money depends upon publicly issued base money in order for it to circulate in the economy. Publicly issued base money circulates in the United States and abroad as coins and Federal Reserve banknotes, and constitute less than 10% of the entire money supply of the United States. Base money in the form of electronic reserves is held in bank accounts of the U.S. Treasury and commercial banks at the Federal Reserve, and in computers at the Federal Reserve. These central bank electronic reserves facilitate the clearing of checks written on demand deposits of privately issued bank debt money.

A check written on bank A and deposited in bank B will only clear if bank A has sufficient central bank reserves at the central bank If bank A does not have enough reserves, it must borrow reserves from another bank, or from the Federal Reserve. If all the private banks in the economy create bank deposit money at about the same rate, then checks written by customers of different banks tend to balance each other during the check clearing process, and very little base money needs to be borrowed to settle the differences in inflow and outflow of reserves at the end of the day. For this reason, a bank must be careful not to expand its lending at a faster rate than other banks, because by doing so its outflow of central bank reserves would be greater than its inflow of central bank reserves. If a bank experiences a net outflow of reserves, and is not able to borrow central bank reserves, then such a bank will become insolvent. Thus, although a private bank can create bank debt money, it is possible that it may fail if it expands its lending faster than other banks. As John Maynard Keynes explained in his Treatise on Money in 1930:

"It is evident that there is no limit to the amount of bank money which the banks can safely create provided they move forward in step. Every movement forward by an individual bank weakens it, but every such movement by one of its neighbour banks strengthens it; so that if all move forward together, no one is weakened on balance. Thus the behaviour of each bank, though it cannot afford to move more than a step in advance of the others, will be governed by the average behaviour of the banks as a whole - to which average, however, it is able to contribute its quota small or large. Each Bank Chairman sitting in his parlour may regard himself as the passive instrument of outside forces over which he has no control; yet the 'outside forces' may be nothing but himself and his fellow-chairmen, and certainly not his depositors."

When bank debt money is loaned into existence by private commercial banks, only the principal amount of the loan is created as bank debt money. Because interest accumulates over a period of time, the interest needed to service the loan is not created at the time the loan is made. At the time of making the loan, accumulated interest is zero. Therefore, it is not possible for a private bank to create the interest at the time a loan is made. The interesting question that automatically arises is this: Where does the money to pay the interest on the debt come from?

The interest needed to service loans comes primarily from that part of the money supply that no longer needs to be repaid as debt. For example, a salary or commission is money that has been earned, not borrowed. Debt based money that was initially borrowed becomes debt free money when it passes into the hands of people whose assets are greater than their liabilities. Although the public is currently highly indebted, the fact remains that the number of people with positive net worth in the U.S. has been increasing. People with positive net worth have assets and cash balances that are debt free. Assets that have been paid for can be sold for cash which would then represent debt free money. Just as money is continually created by banks as debt, money in the form of commissions, salaries, profits, dividends, social security payments, disability payments, etc., is continually accumulating in the hands of people who do not have to use that money to repay debt.

According to the 2015 Financial Report of the U.S. Government, net government spending for the fiscal year 2015 was $3.9 trillion, of which 27% was for Health and Human Services, 24% was for Social Security, 15% was for Defense, 6% was for interest payments on Treasury securities, 4% was for Veteran Affairs, and 24% for all others. The recipients of this $3.9 in government spending received the entire amount of $3.9 trillion as income in the fiscal year 2016. If necessary, some of this money could be used by its recipients to pay the interest on any outstanding debt obligations to private banks, or some of it could be spent by its recipients in other ways, in which case some of the money from government spending would pass into the hands of those who need it to be able to make interest payments or monthly debt payments with it to banks.

According to the website of the Board of Governors of the Federal

Reserve System, there was approximately $1.56 trillion of U.S. dollars in circulation, of which $1.52 trillion was in Federal Reserve notes, that is M0 was $1.56 trillion. According to the website of the Federal Reserve Bank of St. Louis, on July 17, 2017:

M1 (cash + demand deposits + traveler's checks) = $3.4867 trillion

M2 (M1 + savings deposits + CDs < $100,000 + NOW accounts = $13.6083 trillion

Total of demand deposits = $1.3838 trillion

The amount of money that was borrowed into existence as demand deposits was $1.3838 trillion, and the amount of money in cash and travelers checks was $3.4867 - $1.3838 = $2.1028 trillion as of July 17, 2017. Therefore, as of July 17, 2017, the amount of money that depositors were holding in savings deposits, CDs less than $100,000, NOW accounts, and other money market accounts, was $13.6083 - $2.1028 = $11.5055, which is more than eight times the amount of demand deposits. Private commercial banks may be collecting interest on money that they have created out of thin air, but they are also paying interest to depositors holding money in various kinds of savings accounts.

In the current monetary system, most of the money supply as represented by M2 is not being used to exchange goods and services, because most of it is accumulating in savings deposits, CDs, NOW accounts, and money market funds. Therefore, nationalizing the monetary system is not an effective solution to the problem of how to increase the GDP of the United States. Nationalizing the Federal Reserve banks and all the private commercial banks in the country will not increase the velocity of circulation of the traditional U.S. dollar.

If the U.S. government uses a demurrage charged money to spend its money, then the recipients of this money will not be able to hoard demurrage money in interest bearing bank accounts or other types of interest bearing financial instruments. In the current single currency monetary system, government spending is causing a flow of income into interest bearing accounts, which may be good for the recipients of government spending, but is not good for the economy as a whole. Government spending that does not lead to increased spending in the economy cannot generate additional tax revenues for the government.

There is not much difference between a publicly issued currency and a privately issued currency in a single currency monetary system, because the end result is the same - no increase in the velocity of circulation of the currency. A publicly issued demurrage currency such as the Smart dollar will be quite different from the privately issued money lent into existence by private commercial banks. The smart dollar will be able to increase the GDP of the United States, and at the same time produce 'tax' revenues by taxing money instead of income

# THE DUAL CURRENCY MONETARY REFORM PROPOSAL

A completely electronic demurrage charged fiat currency called the Smart dollar will be established as a second national currency for the United States. The Smart dollar will be a fully independent, and freely convertible national currency that will coexist in parallel with the conventional U.S. dollar.

Only the Federal Reserve will be able to create the fiat Smart dollar, out of nothing, by typing in numbers into a computer just as it currently creates the conventional fiat U.S. dollar, ex nihilo, that is, out of nothing, by typing numbers into a computer. Private banks will continue to create traditional U.S. dollars out of nothing through the practice of fractional reserve banking, but private commercial banks will not be allowed to create Smart dollars.

The Smart dollar will only exist in electronic form; the Smart dollar will not exist physically as cash currency. Smart dollars will be held in bank accounts that are distinct and separate from conventional bank accounts holding traditional U.S. dollars. Transactions in Smart dollars will be carried out using cash cards, just as transactions are carried out at the present time using credit and debit cards.

The U.S. Treasury will be allowed to issue a new kind of interest free Treasury bond called a called a sovereign bond which will neither pay interest, nor have a maturity date. The holder of a sovereign bond will be able to 'cash' a sovereign bond at any time by placing the sovereign bond in a demurrage checking account. There will be no demurrage fees levied on a sovereign bond, but the moment a sovereign bond is 'cashed' by placing it in a demurrage checking account, it will be subject to demurrage charges.

The Federal Reserve will provide fiat Smart dollars to the U.S. Treasury in exchange for sovereign bonds, just as it currently provides fiat U.S. dollars to the Treasury in exchange for Treasury bonds, notes, and bills. The amount of Treasury securities that the Federal Reserve can buy directly from the U.S. Treasury is currently limited by law, but the Treasury gets around this limit by selling government bonds to the public and to banks, which the Federal Reserve purchases later in open market operations. There will be no limit on the amount of sovereign bonds that the Federal Reserve can buy directly from the U.S. Treasury.

The Federal Reserve will also provide Smart dollars to private commercial banks for the purpose of lending. The U.S. Treasury can spend Smart dollars into the economy in payment of its debts and obligations. The U.S. Treasury will also be allowed to lend Smart dollars through private commercial banks or other financial institutions. For payment of obligations denominated in conventional U.S. dollars, the U.S. Treasury will be able to exchange Smart dollars for conventional U.S. dollars in currency exchange markets.

The demand for Smart dollars will probably outstrip the supply of Smart dollars, because borrowers will prefer interest free Smart dollar loans to interest bearing conventional dollar loans. It is very likely that the Smart dollar will be worth more than the traditional dollar in currency exchange markets where the two national, but independent currencies will be freely traded. Both from the borrower's and the lender's perspective, an interest free smart loan will be far superior to a conventional dollar loan. The borrower will get drastically lower interest payments, while the U.S. Treasury will receive demurrage revenue, which is really a 'tax' on money.

Smart dollars that have already been created by the Federal Reserve will be lent into the economy through private commercial banks who will be paid an origination fee for administering and servicing Smart dollar loans. Private banks will be able to lend preexisting Smart dollars, but will not be able to loan Smart dollars into existence. Thus, private financial institutions will be brokers, but not creators of Smart dollars.

There will be two kinds of bank accounts to hold Smart dollars. Smart dollars in a demurrage checking account will incur a demurrage fee which be debited electronically at a specified time every day. Smart dollars in a savings account must be placed for at least one year to avoid demurrage fees. It will be possible to move Smart dollars from a savings account to a checking account, but there will be a penalty for doing so before the one year period. If Smart dollars are moved from a savings to a checking account prematurely, then the demurrage fees that would have otherwise accumulated will be levied the instant Smart dollars are moved from a savings to a checking account.

The Board of Governors of the Federal Reserve System will set the rate of demurrage on Smart dollars in the U.S. economy. If the demurrage rate is set at 10% per year, then each Smart dollar in every checking account in the economy will be electronically debited 10/365 = 0.028% every day at a specified time. Demurrage charges can be avoided by a holder of Smart dollars by spending the money before the demurrage fee is applied, in which case the new owner of the Smart dollars will incur the fee. Demurrage fees can be shifted from one person to another, but someone will have to pay a demurrage fee on every Smart dollar in the economy every day.

Monetary reform that establishes the Smart dollar will clearly specify that all demurrage revenues belong to the U.S. government, not to the Federal Reserve System. All demurrage revenue will be credited instantly to a demurrage checking account belonging to the U.S. Treasury. If the demurrage rate is 10%, and if there are ten trillion Smart dollars in the U.S. economy, then one trillion Smart dollars will flow into the coffers of the U.S. Treasury every single year.

The Smart dollar will be an interest free electronic currency, permanently bearing an interest rate of zero. It will not be possible to set a positive or a negative rate of interest to the Smart dollar. A loan denominated in Smart dollars will consequently be an interest free loan. A borrower of an interest free Smart loan will only pay back the principal amount of the loan.

Despite the fact that a borrower of a loan denominated in Smart dollars will only pay back the principal amount of the loan, a Smart dollar loan will generate far more revenues than a conventional interest bearing loan. As soon as the proceeds of a Smart dollar loan is placed in a demurrage checking account, demurrage charges will immediately apply. This means that in addition to the principal amount of the loan, the loan will generate demurrage revenue for the U.S. Treasury indefinitely. The stream of demurrage revenue will not stop after the loan has been repaid, but will continue indefinitely as the original amount of the smart loan circulates in smart checking accounts in the U.S. economy.

Although the Smart dollar cannot have a negative rate of interest, it will be possible to originate Smart dollar loans with a built in incentive of principal reduction, such that with every on time monthly payment of the smart loan, the borrower will get a reduction of, say 1% of the remaining principal balance. In other words, borrowers of smart loans will be rewarded with a reduction of the remaining amount that they owe on the smart loan. This kind of a smart loan will be just like a conventional loan with a negative rate of interest, because the borrower of a Smart dollar loan will pay back less than the principal amount of the loan. Therefore, it will be possible to design a Smart dollar loan such that it will have the same outcome as that of a negative interest loan, without actually setting a negative rate of interest.

The Smart dollar will not be created by loaning it into existence. Just as the Federal Reserve creates, out of nothing, electronic central bank reserves of the U.S. dollar, it will similarly create, out of nothing, electronic Smart dollars as a fiat currency. However, unlike the current conventional dollar which is a non demurrage currency, the Federal Reserve will create the Smart dollar as a demurrage charged currency with a rate of demurrage that has been set by the Board of Governors of the Federal Reserve System.

Because the Smart dollar will not be lent into existence, repayment of a Smart dollar loan will not destroy an amount of Smart dollar equal to the original smart loan. Smart dollars cannot be destroyed by repayment of Smart dollar loans. The Smart dollars that have been repaid can be spent into the economy or lent again to other borrowers. The total amount of Smart dollars in the economy will not shrink unless the Federal Reserve or the U.S. Treasury makes a conscious decision to reduce the supply of Smart dollars by refraining from spending or lending Smart dollars. The money supply of traditional U.S. dollars contracts during a recession, but the amount of Smart dollars will not automatically shrink during a recession or an economic downturn.

The money certificates proposed in the Bankhead-Pettengill bill of 1933 were self liquidating because they would be destroyed after they were redeemed for U.S. dollars by the United States Postal Service. Unlike those proposed money certificates, the Smart dollar will not be self liquidating. The fact that the Smart dollar will not exist as paper currency means that no postage stamps will be needed to keep this currency valid as legal tender. An automatic electronic debit of the demurrage fee in a demurrage checking account will keep the Smart dollar valid as legal tender in perpetuity. Demurrage revenues will flow to the Treasury, hence the total amount of Smart dollars in the economy will not be reduced by demurrage, unless the U.S. Treasury makes a conscious decision not to spend or lend the demurrage revenues that it will be receiving.

The proposed demurrage charged national complementary currency offers some powerful monetary tools that are not available in the current single currency monetary system of the United States. For the first time in the history of the United States, the United States will have a demurrage charged national currency that will primarily serve as a medium of exchange. If the United States wants to stimulate the economy through a greater exchange of goods and services, then it will have the power to do so by spending Smart dollars into the economy, because unlike the conventional dollar, the Smart dollar is not likely to be hoarded.

U.S. dollars can be dropped from helicopters, but people on the ground who collect those dollars as they fall from the sky, may not want to spend those dollars. They may choose to hoard those dollars. Smart dollars cannot be dropped from the sky, but they can surely be credited to a holder's demurrage checking account. Unlike someone who collects conventional dollars dropped from a helicopter, a recipient of Smart dollars will be far more motivated to spend the Smart dollars before the balance of the amount of Smart dollars in his checking account gets reduced by demurrage fees.

The rate of demurrage set by the Board of Governors of the Federal Reserve will itself be another powerful monetary tool at the disposal of the Federal Reserve. The rate of demurrage is similar to the gas pedal of a car which can accelerate the speed of the car. If an increase in the velocity of the Smart dollar is desired, the rate of demurrage can be increased. If the velocity of the Smart dollar seems to be overheating the economy, the rate of demurrage can be lowered.

Since the U.S. dollar exists physically, a negative rate of interest cannot be set by the Federal Reserve, even in an economic downturn, when a negative rate of interest is absolutely necessary. Setting interest rates on the Smart dollar will not be possible because it will be a non interest bearing currency, but the outcome of a negative rate of interest can be realized by originating Smart dollar loans with the built in feature of principal reduction.

# CONCLUSION

According to the Congressional Budget Office, the federal budget deficit is projected to increase from $559 billion in 2017 to $1,297 billion in 2026, while the interest payment on the federal debt is projected to increase from $270 billion in 2017 to $714 billion in 2016. This astronomical rise in both the level of the federal deficit, and the amount of interest payment necessary to service the federal debt in the year 2026, poses a mortal threat to the financial system and the economy of the United States in less than ten years from now. The United States economy is on the brink of a precipice.

As I have elaborated in this book, it is not possible to ward off the possibility of a default on the national debt with the use of conventional methods such as cutting spending, or raising tax rates, or devaluing the dollar, or increasing the gross domestic product. Government revenues simply cannot be increased fast enough to match the increase in the amount of interest payments necessary to service the national debt in 2026, because the growth in gross domestic product is projected to be only around 2.2% in the coming decade. Similarly, government entitlements and other obligations cannot be cut significantly to reduce the federal budget deficits in the coming decade.

The impending disaster of a default on the national debt can be averted only by the use of an unconventional solution to the conventional problem of an unsustainable interest burden. An altogether different approach is required to solve the problem of the mounting interest burden on federal debt, which is fast becoming unsustainable. To eliminate the possibility of a default on Treasury debt, we need to reform the current monetary system of the United States.

If we carefully examine the nature of the U.S. dollar that is currently in place, we will find that there is a serious flaw in our monetary system which needs to be corrected through appropriate monetary reform. The U.S. dollar cannot perform the role of a medium of exchange and the role of a convenient store of value simultaneously, because these two roles are in contradiction with each other. There is no escape from the conclusion that it is this defect in our current monetary system that has placed the United States in such a precarious situation.

Incredible as it may seem, there is a way for the United States to avoid a default on its unsustainable interest burden. The problem of the mounting burden of interest payments can be addressed effectively with the establishment of a demurrage charged complementary currency as a second independent currency within the framework of a dual currency monetary system. This can be accomplished without nationalizing the private banking industry, without abolishing fractional reserve banking, and without changing the structure of the Federal Reserve System.

The U.S. economy is in dire need of a fully independent demurrage charged currency that is totally electronic, that is freely convertible in currency exchange markets, and which is allowed to coexist in parallel with the traditional U.S. dollar. A demurrage currency will function primarily as a medium of exchange, and will facilitate the exchange of goods and services in the economy.

The demurrage currency will be source of income for the U.S. government, because demurrage fees will be repatriated to the U.S. Treasury. If the Board of Governors of the Federal Reserve System set the rate of demurrage at 10% per year, it means that the U.S. Treasury will receive 10% of the entire stock of demurrage money in the economy every year as demurrage fees.

This wonderful 'tax' on money, which is what demurrage really is, will be the new source of revenues with which the entire national debt can be paid off in a matter of decades. It will not be necessary to raise additional taxes, nor will it be necessary to cut entitlements. The excruciating burden of interest payments will cease to be a burden!

# BIBLIOGRAPHY

Ahamed, Liaquat (2009) The Bankers Who Broke The World, The Penguin Press, New York

Bagehot, Walter (Reprinted in 2016) Lombard Street, Printed by Createspace, North Charleston

Bernanke, Ben S. (2013) The Federal Reserve And The Financial Crisis, Princeton University Press, Princeton

Boyle, David (2002) The Money Changers, Earthscan Publications Limited, London

Brown, Ellen Hodgson (2008) The Web of Debt, Third Millennium Press, Baton Rouge

Brown, Ellen Hodgson (2013) The Public Bank Solution, Third Millennium Press, Baton Rouge

Catchings, Waddill & Roos, Charles F. (1953) Money, Men and Machines, Little Brown and Company in Association with Duell Sloan & Pearce, Inc.

Cook, Richard C. (2009) We hold These Truths, Tendril Press, Denver

Cavanaugh, Francis X. (1996) The Truth About The National Debt, Harvard Business School Press, Boston, Massachusetts

Creutz, Helmut (2010) The Money Syndrome, Publisher: Adeolu Alao, Northampton, UK

Douglas Clifford Hugh (1920) Economic Democracy, Harcourt, Brace & Howe, New York

Duncan, Richard (2003) The Dollar Crisis, John Wiley & Sons (Asia) Pte Ltd, Singapore

Duncan, Richard (2012) The New depression, John Wiley & Sons Singapore Pte. Ltd.

Eichengreen, Barry (2011) Exorbitant Privilege, Oxford University Press, New York

Fisher, Irving (First Published in 1912; Reprinted in 2007) The Purchasing Power of Money, Cosimo, Inc., New York

Fisher, Irving (2009) 100% Money and the Public Debt, ThaiSunset Publications, Thailand

Friedman, Milton (1994) Money Mischief, Harcourt Brace & Company, New York

Friedman, Milton & Schwartz, Anna Jacobson (1963) A Monetary History of the United States, 1867-1960, Princeton University Press, Princeton

Galbraith, John Kenneth (1975) Money: Whence it Came, Where it went, Houghton Mifflin Company, Boston

Gesell, Silvio (First Published 1936; Reprinted in 2013) The Natural Economic Order, Isha Books, New Delhi, India

Gordon, John Steele (1999) The Great Game, Scribner, New York

Gordon, John Steele (2010) Hamilton's Blessing, Walker & Company, New York

Greider, William (1987) Secrets of the Temple, Simon & Schuster, New York

Griffin, G. Edward (2005) The Creature From Jekyll Island: A Second Look at the Federal Reserve, American Media, Westlake Village, California

Hallsmith, Gwendolyn & Lietaer (2011) Creating Wealth, New Society Publishers, Gabriola Island, British Columbia, Canada

Helleiner, Eric & Kirshner, Jonathan (2009) The Future of the Dollar, Cornell University Press, Ithaca, New York

Hoda, Anjum (2016) Bluff: The Game Central Banks Play and How it Leads to Crisis, Oneworld Publications, London, United Kingdom

Hutchinson, Frances (1998) What Everybody Really Wants to Know About Money, Jon Carpenter Publishing, Oxfordshire, United Kingdom

Jackson, Andrew & Dyson, Ben (2012) Modernising Money, Publisher: Positive Money, London

Kennedy, Margrit (1995) Interest and Inflation Free Money, New Society Publishers, Philadelphia

Kennedy, Margrit with Ehrenschwender, Stephanie (2012) Occupy Money, New Society Publishers, Gabriola Island, British Columbia, Canada

Keynes, John Maynard (1964) The General Theory of Employment, Interest, And Money, Harcourt Brace & Company, New York

Kotlikoff, Laurence J. & Burns, Scott (2005) The Coming Generational Storm, The MIT Press, Cambridge, Massachusetts

Krugman, Paul (2009) The Return of Depression Economics, W.W. Norton & Co New York

Krugman, Paul (2012) End This Depression Now!, W.W. Norton & Company, New York

Lietaer, Bernard (2001) The Future of Money, Century The Random House Group, London, UK

Lietaer, Bernard & Dunne, Jacqui (2013) Berrett-Koehler Publishers, Inc., San Francisco

Lietaer, Bernard, Ulanowicz, Robert & Goerner, Sally (2011) Reinventing Money: An Ecosystematic Approach, pages 79-109, in What Comes After Money, Evolver Editions, Berkeley, California

Lietaer, Bernard & Goerner, Sally & Brunnhuber, Stefan (2012) Triarchy Press, Devon, UK

Lowenstein, Roger (2015) America's Bank, Penguin Press, New York

McKinnon, Ronald I. (2013) The Unloved Dollar Standard, Oxford University Press, New York

Mellor, Mary (2016) Debt or Democracy, Pluto Press, London

Mellor, Mary (2010) The Future of Money, Pluto Press, London

Mann, Catherine L. (1999) Is The U.S. Trade Deficit Sustainable?, Institute For International Economics, Washington, D.C.

Mian, Atif & Sufi, Amir (2014) House of Debt, The University Of Chicago Press, Chicago

Mikuni, Akio & Murphy, R. Taggart (2002) Japan's Policy Trap, Brookings Institution Press, Washington, D.C.

Mullins, Eustace (1991) The Secrets of the Federal Reserve, Bridger House Publishers, Inc., Carson City, Nevada

Newman, Frank N. (2011) Six Myths That Hold America Back, Diversion Books, New York

Newman, Frank N. (2013) Freedom from National Debt, Two Harbors Press, Minneapolis

Nichols, Dorothy M. & Gonczy, Marie L. (1992) Modern Money Mechanics, Federal Reserve Bank of Chicago, Chicago, Illinois

Paul, Ron (2009) End the Fed, Grand Central Publishing, New York

Pettifor, Ann (2017) The Production of Money, Publisher: Verso, London

Rauchway, Eric (2015) The Money Makers, Basic Books, New York

Rickards, James (2011) Currency Wars, Portfolio/Penguin, New York

Rickards, James (2014) The Death of Money, Portfolio/ Penguin, New York

Rogoff, Kenneth S. (2016) The Curse of Cash, Princeton University Press, Princeton

Rothbard, Murray N. (2005) A History of Money and Banking in the United States, Ludwig von Mises Institute, Auburn, Alabama

Rowbotham, Michael (2000) Goodbye America!, Jon Carpenter Publishing, Oxfordshire, UK

Rowbotham, Michael (2007) The Grip of Death, Jon Carpenter Publishing, Oxfordshire, UK

Ryan-Collins, Josh; Greenham, Tony; Werner, Richard & Jackson, Andrew (2011) Where Does Money Come From? The New Economics Foundation, London, Great Britain

Sehgal, Kabir (2015) Coined: The Rich Life of Money And How Its History Has Shaped Us, Grand Central Publishing, New York

Siddiqui, M. Nejatullah (1996) Role of the State in the Economy, The Islamic Foundation, Leiester, United Kingdom

Skidelsky, Robert (2009) Keynes: The Return of the Master, Public Affairs, New York

Steil, Benn (2013) The Battle of Bretton Woods, Princeton University Press, Princeton

Still, Bill (2011) The National Debt, Reinhardt & Still Publishers, St. Petersburg, Florida

Turner, Adair (2016) Between Debt And The Devil, Princeton University Press, Princeton

Warwick, David R. (1998) Ending Cash: The Public Benefits of Federal Electronic Currency, Quorum Books, Westport, Connecticut

Walker, David M. (2009) Comeback America, Random House, New York

Walter, Ingo (1989) The Secret Money Market, Harper Business, Division of Harper Collins

Weatherford, Jack (1997) The History of Money, Crown Publishers, Inc., New York

Wray, L. Randall (1998) Understanding Modern Money, Edward Elgar Publishing, UK

Zarlega, Stephen (2002) The Lost Science of Money, American Monetary Institute, New York

Printed in the United States
By Bookmasters